How
Patience
Works

The Quiet Mind to Benefit Others

Janet Kathleen Ettele

KARUNA PUBLICATIONS

Published in 2014 by Karuna Publications, Inc.
A non-proft 501(c)(3) corporation

Book design by Clare Cerullo

Printed in the United States of America

Library of Congress Cataloging-in-Publication Data is available upon request.

ISBN 978-1-9371140-3-9

www.karunapublications.org

⏜

How Patience Works is the third in the How Life Works series that is drawn from Master Shantideva's teachings contained in *A Guide to the Bodhisattva's Way of Life*. For more information about the How Life Works series and the author, please visit www.janetettele.com

Also Available in the How Life Works Series
How Generosity Works—ISBN 978-0976546986
How the Root of Kindness Works—ISBN 978-1937114046

I dedicate this book with admiration, love, and respect to my teacher, Gyumed Khensur Rinpoche Lobsang Jampa.

When China forcefully invaded Rinpoche's home country of Tibet in 1959, he traveled on foot over the Himalayas into India where he and thousands of other Tibetan refugees have lived in exile.

Never giving rise to anger, even in the face of extreme aggression and cruelty, Rinpoche maintains perfect compassion for those who suffer from violence inflicted by others and those who use violence to harm others.

For nearly six years I have studied with Rinpoche. I continue to marvel at the sheer beauty of a teacher who consistently reflects a lifetime of dedicated study and whose life is a demonstration of mastery of the dharma practice. Remaining steady in his patience, he is tireless in his efforts to promote harmony in the world through his teaching. Rinpoche is indeed a rare and precious gem.

Introduction

A Guide to the Bodhisattva's Way of Life (Bodhichayavatara) was first taught by Master Shantideva in India during the eighth century. He was born a prince, but chose the life of a monk and studied at Nalanda University. While at Nalanda, Master Shantideva appeared to do nothing but sleep, eat, and other necessary functions of the body and was perceived by the other monks to be an embarrassment to their prestigious university. The monks resented him for his laziness, and since there were rules that prevented them from having him expelled, they designed a plan they believed would be a perfect way to shame him into voluntarily leaving Nalanda. The plan included ordering him to give a public teaching. They thought that certainly he would realize that since he knew nothing and had nothing of value to teach, he would run away to avoid humiliation.

In the center of a field, they prepared a very high throne for him to teach from and invited people from all the surrounding areas to attend. To increase the challenge, they asked him to teach something that had never been taught before. Determined to leave no stone unturned in their effort to humiliate him, they had built the throne with no stairs by which to reach its seat. When Shantideva approached the throne, he placed his hand on its side and was immediately transported to the seat of the throne. Then, Shantideva proceeded to speak eloquently and spontaneously, reciting the Bodhichayavatara, which is now one of the most renowned texts in Buddhism. To the astonishment of those in attendance, the profound teaching flowed from Shantideva in the form of song-like poetry. It has been said that when Master Shantideva reached the final chapter on the Perfection of Wisdom, that his body raised higher and higher from the seat of the throne until he eventually disappeared from sight. His teaching continued but was only heard by those who having attained higher realizations in their own minds had the ability to hear.

A *Guide to the Bodhisattva's Way of Life* has provided students of the Buddhist Dharma from that day forward with a clear and wisdom filled path on how to practice what is commonly known as the Six Paramitas, or the Six Perfections. The Six Perfections provide the necessary guidance on how a Bodhisattva, motivated by compassion and the intention to benefit all beings, must perfect his or her mind on the path to enlightenment. For ordinary people like most of us, the verses provide the perfect guidance to live happy and meaningful lives.

How Patience Works is based on the third perfection of Master Shantideva's *Guide to the Bodhhisattva's Way of Life*, the Perfection of Patience. There are three types of Patience: Patience with those who harm you; Patience with your own suffering; and Patience with your spiritual practice. Focusing the mind through contemplation of the teaching, and meditation to keep a peaceful mind, the practice of Patience is the antidote to anger. Through this practice one comes to understand that there is no true enemy other than ignorance, the root cause of anger. Cultivating wisdom (understanding the true nature of how things exist) facilitates the most powerful antidote to anger by destroying ignorance at its root.

The challenging circumstances we meet in daily life provide the perfect opportunity to apply this practice. As our understanding deepens and our practice strengthens we experience its peaceful result. We begin to see that regardless of faith or tradition, true peace is not naïve optimism but an achievable reality that begins with a wise and compassionate mind.

I have written this book with a heart-filled wish for peace in the world and with the highest respect and gratitude for the generations of teachers who have made great sacrifices in their own lives to preserve the teachings.

Suppose someone should awaken from a dream
In which they experienced
one hundred years of happiness,
And suppose another should awaken from a dream
In which they experienced
just one moment of happiness;

For both of these people who have awoken,
That happiness will never return.
Similarly, whether my life has been long or short,
At the time of death it will be finished like this.
VI. 57, 58

My Darling,

This morning a strong wind stirred the branches by our bedroom window. Sometimes the wind moves through the forest as a gentle song in its leaves, and sometimes as a violent and destructive storm. So it is with the mind. It can move us to be a gentle and loving presence or a force of violence and destruction. May all understand this simple truth and take great care to generate only peace.

Always grateful for your wise, gentle, and loving presence, I am missing you now.

Love Always,
Esther

How Patience Works

It was the month of May when the New England land-scape was drenched in every shade of green a color wheel can spin. The morning sun rose a little hotter in a golden sky, and winter was a memory washed away by warm, humid breezes that spread dogwood blossoms instead of snowflakes.

Troy worked fast, clearing tables to keep up with customers coming through the wooden screen door that creaked when it opened and snapped when it sprang shut. The windows were raised and ceiling fans whirred, mixing scents of bacon, maple syrup, and coffee with the lilacs that were in full bloom outside the diner. It was the busiest time of morning when voices competing to be heard grew loud.

Working with Maggie was the best part of Troy's job. Even though it had been only six months, Troy felt as if they had known each other forever. Her smile and the sound of her voice still hadn't lost their power to beat a new rhythm into his heart.

"Mrs. Sternau wants more coffee, Mags," Troy said as he squeezed between tables, carrying a tray full of dishes.

It was easy to find Mrs. Sternau. She sat at the same table where she had spent every Thursday morning for years. It was the corner table next to the window where a red rose in a bud vase was perched on its sill. Wearing a shawl woven in coral and cream, and her white hair pinned into an elegant twist, Mrs. Sternau smiled as Maggie approached her table.

"Thank you, dear." She sat with her hands folded in her lap, and a napkin spread neatly over her skirt while Maggie refilled her cup with steaming black coffee. "Would you please bring my check?"

"Yes, of course," Maggie answered. "I'll get it for you now."

Mrs. Sternau sipped her coffee, watching the activity in the diner until her eyes rested on the empty chair opposite her. Placing her cup in its saucer, she closed her eyes and filled the empty chair with the image her memory preferred. In this way her husband could sit as real as life itself, wearing his herringbone blazer with the glasses case clipped into the front pocket. In her mind, she and Albert were talking quietly together over breakfast. It could have been a conversation about an exceptional student in his class or the weekend drive they would take to visit their grandchildren.

Not wanting to startle her, Maggie spoke softly, "Here's your check, Mrs. Sternau. Have a nice day."

"Thank you…is it Molly?" she asked.

"No," Maggie replied with a smile. This question had become routine. "I'm Maggie."

"Oh yes, of course." Mrs. Sternau laughed. "I'll get it straight one of these days!" She opened her purse and took a ten-dollar bill from her wallet and handed it to Maggie along with the check. When she finished her coffee, she folded her napkin and dabbed the corners of her mouth. She reached for the cane that leaned against the wall beside her and stood, balancing carefully before walking steadily to the door.

Troy had noticed her preparing to leave and went ahead to open the door. "Goodbye, Mrs. Sternau," he said. "Have a nice day."

"Thank you, Trevor." She stopped in the doorway and looked intently at Troy. "It's a marvelous day today; I wish you a very nice day as well."

Troy accepted whatever name she came up with. Sometimes it was Timothy or Teddy, but lately it was Trevor. No matter what, she managed to find a name that began with T. He had a soft spot for Mrs. Sternau, especially since he discovered the messages she left written in beautiful script on the scallop-edged paper placemats. Typically they were thoughtful reflections or fragments from a conversation she might have had with her husband.

Theo the cook told Troy that before her husband died, the couple came for breakfast every Thursday morning. He died many years earlier during his sleep. At his funeral, in addition to his family, the church was filled with students, professors from the university, local friends, and old friends who had traveled north from their previous home in Maryland. There were members of clergy wearing customary black and white and Buddhist monks in maroon and yellow robes. The staff and regular customers from the diner came too. With so many people from so many walks of life, Theo said it was one of the more memorable funerals he had ever been to.

Professor Sternau was known for his brilliant mind and for a distinctive teaching style that inspired students. Recognizing that defending their views was an effective way to keep students engaged in learning, he welcomed lively debates in his class. As far as Mrs. Sternau was concerned, he was the absolute cream of her life. After his death she grieved with stoic dignity and continued doing many of the things they had enjoyed together, Thursday mornings at the diner being one of them.

Dearest,

This morning's lilacs fill the air with sweet perfume, but their blossoms will soon fade into memory stored in the soil, feeding the roots for future blossoms. I hold the memory of you softly and tenderly, like the soil holds the delicate petals of the lilacs. By the way, the garden is now in bloom, displaying the magnificence of each moment you spent tending it.

Adoringly,
Esther

Troy read Mrs. Sternau's message and then folded the paper placemat and put it in his pocket. He couldn't simply toss her messages into the bus pans along with dirty dishes, silverware, and napkins. A library of coffee-stained placemats was filling his dresser drawer at home. When Troy first found Mrs. Sternau's notes, he felt a touch of awkwardness as if he were eavesdropping on a private conversation. But he decided she wouldn't have left the notes on the table if they weren't for reading. Sometimes, when Troy longed for inspiration or wisdom, he reached into the drawer to randomly select one of her placemat messages. It didn't seem to matter which one he opened; in each he found a strong voice of wisdom that inevitably provided just what he needed.

Mrs. Sternau's messages fit right in with the unusual sequence of chance meetings that had begun to reshape Troy's world since he had come home from college. His fall semester had been a waste of drinking more than studying, and he had a string of failing grades to show for it. He returned home ashamed, unsettled, and resentful. But he learned that every now and then good luck waits like a precious dormant seed within unlucky circumstances.

His first good luck came through Grace, the music teacher, and then through Abe, a Vietnam veteran. Each had presented special wisdom and guidance to handle life's rough patches with skill and compassion. Troy sensed he was on a profound journey that was unfolding with a design he was both creating and discovering. The day Maggie introduced him to Abe, the owner of her favorite second-hand shop, it became clear that she was the perfect companion for this journey. With the wisdom of hindsight, he wouldn't have exchanged stellar grades for all he was learning, especially through getting to know Grace and Abe.

Maggie liked to tease Troy about what she said was an obsession with Mrs. Sternau's letters. The truth was that Maggie looked forward to reading them too. During one of the past winter's snowstorms, Troy took a small box of her messages to Maggie's house when he went to spend the day with her. As snow piled into drifts outside, they camped out in Maggie's living room draped in colorful crocheted blankets on the plaid sofa she had found in Abe's shop. Reading from folded placemats taken from the box, some of the messages prompted more conversation than others. Within them all was the essence of wisdom coupled with a deep love that had shared a lifetime, and where death seemed only another landscape Mrs. Sternau had found a way to navigate.

"Did she leave another note?" Maggie asked.

"Yup, she did." Troy was carrying a highchair to a table where a family was trying to settle a crying toddler. "I'll show it to you after work."

"Great." Maggie looked at the line of people still waiting for tables. "It looks like that might be awhile."

⌒

Even if it were the nature of the childish
To cause harm to other beings,
It would still be incorrect to be angry with them,
For this would be like begrudging fire for having the
nature to burn.

And even if the fault were temporary
In they who are by nature reliable,
It would still be incorrect to be angry,
For this would be like begrudging space for allowing
smoke to arise in it.
VI. 39, 40

By the time the counters, tables, and floor had been cleaned, and the condiment jars and salt and pepper-shakers refilled, Maggie and Troy couldn't wait to leave the diner behind. They walked into the afternoon sun that shined lace shadows onto the pavement where Troy's blue truck was parked. Troy opened the doors to release the heat.

"Let's go over there and have lunch while the truck cools off," he said, pointing to a rock at the edge of the parking lot. Carrying the bagged lunch Theo had given them, they walked to the wide sloping rock where specks of mica sparkled sunlight under the shade.

Maggie opened the paper wrapping of her sandwich and spread it across her lap. "So, what pearls of wisdom did Mrs. Sternau write today?" she asked, lightly lifting the top layer of bread to check its contents.

"Here you go." Troy handed the folded placemat to Maggie. He watched her eyes follow the words on the paper as she read the message and then lift to meet his own.

"Oh my God," she said. "This is beautiful. I love the part about the memory of the flowers being stored in the soil." And then she read aloud, *"The garden is now in bloom, displaying the magnificence of each moment you spent tending it."* She handed the creased placemat back to Troy and sighed. "Isn't it just so sad? She misses her husband so much."

"I know," Troy agreed. "But everyone will eventually be in the same boat if they live long enough." Troy reread the note before folding it back into his shirt pocket. "I just hope if I make it to that point that I'll somehow have the wisdom and courage Mrs. Sternau has."

"You will, Troy," Maggie said as she watched a young mother balance a baby on her hip while keeping a tight hold on her little boy's hand. The boy was tugging her to chase pigeons feasting on the bread Theo had tossed into the parking lot. "I have absolutely no doubt that you will."

"Well," Troy said, "for now I just need to muster the courage to finish out the classes I'm taking. Even if I get my grades up, I've decided not to go back to school in New Hampshire."

"Really?"

"Yeah, Maggie." Troy finished the last of the chips and put the empty package into the lunch bag. "Even dealing with Maureen has had its plusses. I'm actually really loving being back here."

Maureen was the woman Troy's father married after he left Troy's mother and their family. Although his dad felt that leaving his wife didn't equal leaving his family, Troy's experience had been different.

"Amazing things are happening here," Troy said. "I know it's still the same town I grew up in, but it's like a new world for me." He considered saying something more before continuing, "Mags, we both saw our parents bail on marriage, and we know better than to rely on some idea of forever and ever. But I really do love you and see no reason to go away unless you're coming with me."

"I feel the same way, Troy." It wasn't that she felt she had to just say something nice in return; Maggie didn't say things she didn't mean. "I'm really happy you aren't leaving."

"Me too." Troy finished his lunch and sat quietly, gazing at the hills on the horizon while a soft breeze spun clouds into wisps.

"Do you feel like taking a ride to the beach?" he asked.

"Sure," she said. "But the water's still too cold to swim."

"You never know," Troy smiled. "Let's stop by my house to get some towels just in case." He hesitated and then added, "On second thought, let's not. I don't want to hear Maureen get all crazy about bringing sand in the house when I get home."

Even though insights gained from Grace and Abe improved their relationship, Troy walked on eggshells around Maureen's moods. Living with his father and

Maureen was a mixed bag of easing his financial strain from college debt and tolerating Maureen's neurotic outbursts. Grace taught him a meditation practice that focused on compassion to help bring peace to his mind. The practice also brought a softening in the dynamics between him and Maureen. It wasn't exactly a jovial relationship, but at least it had begun to warm into something more pleasant. And since he kept a full schedule working at the diner, taking night classes, and spending time with Maggie, their paths didn't have to cross so often.

"If you really think you might swim, my roommates and I have beach towels at our house. Let's stop by there on our way."

⌒

Whatever befalls me,
I shall not disturb my mental joy;
For having been made unhappy,
I shall not accomplish what I wish,
And my virtues will decline.

Why be unhappy about something
If it can be remedied?

And what is the use of being unhappy about something
If it cannot be remedied?
VI. 9, 10

They tossed an old comforter into the back of Troy's truck and filled a cooler with water, nectarines, and a bag of popcorn. Having traded their sneakers for flip-flops and their jeans for shorts, they drove with the windows down, following the road that wound through long stretches of woods and passed between two lakes. Fishermen stood in isolated distance from one another, patiently casting their lines into the water.

Maggie turned to watch them fish as they drove past the lakes. "I'd never want to put a worm on a hook or even catch a fish, but there's something about fishing that looks really appealing," she said. "I mean, it's like you can feel purposeful even if all you're doing is enjoying a nice day and a pretty view."

"Maggie," Troy said, "if you don't want to bait a hook or catch a fish, then you don't just hang out with an empty line dangling in the water—there's no purpose in that!"

"Well, I know," she agreed. "But so what?"

"Okay," he said, "when we get to the beach, I'll find you a stick and a string, and you can pretend you're fishing so you don't feel like you're wasting time doing nothing."

Maggie ignored his remark and moved on to see what CDs Troy had in the glove box. Sifting through a short stack of plastic cases, she settled on The Grateful Dead, loaded the CD into the player, and turned up the volume.

⌣

Troy believed that there are certain ingredients that make for a perfect day, and they were all present in that moment: blue skies, beautiful scenery, Maggie sitting next to him, and some of his favorite music. Life was good, and he was happy.

When Troy first came home from New Hampshire, he never anticipated a day this joyful could be six months in his future. He didn't imagine that caring and wise people such as Grace or Abe existed. And he certainly didn't expect a twenty-five-hundred-year-old lineage of Buddhist wisdom to change the way he experienced his own life.

Grace taught him about karma and the importance of motivation and intention. She taught him that compassion isn't only for your favorite people in life, but also for people like Maureen who seem intent on causing you pain. When we offer compassion without discrimination, including to the people we are challenged by, we also discover one of the keys to our own true happiness.

Abe showed Troy that even with his troubled history that included things like drinking too much and getting into fights, there were ways to transform the impact of his past and redirect his future. By orienting his mind to the interdependence of all things in life, things he might do, say, or think could be considered through an entirely different system that understood the deeper function of cause and effect.

Troy remembered the first afternoon he took Natalie to her piano lesson. He had just returned home from college somewhat numb and feeling very alone. Driving Natalie was at least a reason to get out the door, and her cheerful innocence was easy to be around. Natalie was born shortly after his father married Maureen. The dread of a half sibling had the surprising outcome of a little sister who simply adored him and whom he loved with all the fullness an older brother can offer.

Grace invited him to look through her bookshelf while he waited for Natalie to have her lesson. He was drawn to a book cover of a Buddha in a tranquil garden and began reading. When Grace noticed his interest, she suggested he take the book home with him. Since steering clear of Maureen had been his best survival tactic, he spent a lot of time in his room reading the book or playing his guitar. Later, when he told Grace that he hoped to take music classes at school, she offered to teach him music theory so he could meet the requirements to enroll. Between discussions about music and things Troy was reading in the book, a comfortable sense of trust and caring developed between them. So much so that Troy told her about the challenges he was facing at home. Maybe it was her musical ear that tuned into the nuances of the things he said, prompting her to say the things he most needed to hear.

When Troy found a Gibson Les Paul guitar in Abe's shop, Abe offered him a deal. If he would help him with a couple of days' work moving the contents from a house into his shop, he could have the vintage guitar.

Working with Abe, Troy learned about the life-altering experiences Abe had in Vietnam and how he managed to find peace after the nightmares of war followed him home. He also learned the extreme importance of mindfulness. Not in the casual way the word is often tossed around, but about being vigilantly mindful of actions of thought, speech, and body with a full understanding of the results each action sets in motion. Troy found the value of his time with Abe far exceeded that of the guitar. The value was in the knowledge he took home with him after the job was done and in the friendship of a man who demonstrated courage unlike anyone he'd ever known.

The road followed some bends and curves past saltbox houses and over a stone bridge. As they made the turn toward the beach, the salty smell of seaweed and low tide filled the air.

"Oh no," Maggie's voice broke through the music. "It's low tide."

"That's okay," Troy said. "That just means it's coming back in."

Maggie smiled. "You've become quite the optimist, haven't you?"

"Ya think?" Troy asked, enjoying how much he and things in his life had changed.

Should one person ignorantly do wrong,
And another ignorantly become angry (with the
wrongdoer),
Who would be at fault?
And who would be without fault?

Why did I previously commit those actions,
Because of which, others now cause me harm?
Since everything is related to my actions,
Why should I bear malice towards these (enemies)?

When I have seen this to be so,
I should strive for what is meritorious
(In order to) certainly bring about
Loving thoughts between all.
VI. 67,68,69

There was an acoustical change when they left the
pavement behind and stepped into the warm sand that
shifted and sank under their feet. The wind skimmed
the surface of the water and brushed their faces with
thick salty tones. The calls of the seagulls circling the
water and combing the beach filled the air with an un-
changed language from a distant time.

Maggie kicked off her flip-flops and carried them along with the blanket, while Troy managed the cooler and towels. Evaluating where the tide would rise, marked by strewn clusters of seaweed and shells, they surveyed the beach to choose a place to put their blanket and cooler.

Flip-flops in hand, Maggie pointed to an open patch of sand near the jetty of rocks that bordered the beach. "That looks like a good spot."

"Looks good to me," Troy agreed.

They walked past an older couple sitting in folding chairs under a blue and pink striped beach umbrella. Engrossed in the books they held in their laps, they were undisturbed by seagulls that encroached into the periphery of their beach blanket and by the sand that sprinkled on it when Troy's flip-flops kicked sand in his wake.

Maggie and Troy spread their blanket, settling it in the breeze before lowering it onto the sand. Leaving their cooler, towels, and sandals on the blanket, they walked gingerly around beach rocks and shells to the water's edge to put their feet in the water.

"Good Lord, it's freezing. It's definitely too cold to swim." Maggie stepped back onto the sand where her feet could soak in the warmth deposited by the sun.

"I don't know about that," Troy leaned down to put his hands in the water. "It's not that bad." He shook the water from his hands and wiped them dry on his shorts. He began lifting stones, looking for just the right shape and size for skipping. "Watch this, Mags." He curved his index finger around a stone, drew his arm back, and with just the right motion from his wrist sent the stone skipping against the current of the water. He watched and counted as the stone bounced six times before sinking. "I'm a little rusty, but I've still got it." He searched the beach for more stones, and when he found one that was smooth and flat, he offered it to Maggie.

Maggie positioned the stone in her hand. "I was never very good at this; it's always hit or miss for me." She sent the stone off to skip twice before it sank.

They walked along the shoreline, absorbed in the sound of gulls and tide, picking up stones and skipping them into the water. After a few half-hearted attempts at skipping stones, Maggie began searching for shells and rocks to take home with her. She especially liked rocks with interesting bands or specks of color, and she kept them at home in glass jars and bowls filled with water so their designs wouldn't fade in the dry air. One of these days she thought she might string necklaces or maybe even earrings with the smaller shells that had holes worn through them. Soon her hands and pockets were filled, and she walked back to the patch of beach she and Troy had claimed with their blanket. Sitting next to the small pile of shells she had emptied from her pockets, she began sifting the sand next to the blanket, searching for more. It wasn't long before Troy took a seat next to her.

Brushing the sand from his feet, he asked "Hey, Mags, do you ever think about what you were doing, like maybe a year ago, and realize that none of what you're doing now even existed in your mind as a thought?"

"What do you mean?"

"Like last year, Maggie," Troy began. "I've told you about the bad stretch I went through after Jason was killed and Cecile broke up with me." A speeding car hit Jason one night when he was walking home. Even after attending the wake and funeral, Troy simply could not accept that Jason would never show up in his life again. They had grown up together like brothers and understood each other so well that even the more painful things in life were softened by love and laughter. Sometimes, when Troy was sleeping, Jason would visit him in his dreams. Although he rarely talked about it, Troy was convinced these dream visits were actual visits. They would hug and laugh, and then Jason would simply vanish the way dream images do.

"I haven't told you everything about what went down during that time, Maggie, but there's some stuff I feel you should know." He picked up a fistful of sand and funneled it loosely over the open palm of his other hand. "I used to drink a lot. Um… I mean, probably no more than the other people I was hanging out with at school, but definitely more than the kids who were actually taking school seriously." As he continued to sieve the sand he poured over his hand, he plucked out tiny shells and added them to Maggie's collection. "But after Jason was killed, I crossed the line into another kind of drinking. I'm not altogether clear how it happened, but I wasn't just drinking to party and have a good time anymore. I was so angry and so sad that it was as if my drinking was driven by something like not being able to handle being in my own skin." He laughed a little nervously. He didn't like those memories, but he loved and respected Maggie and didn't want to feel as if he was carrying a dark and secret past into their relationship. He had thought about it long and hard and considered that he didn't have to spill every little transgression of his past, but if there was something that was still impacting his present, then he didn't want to distort their relationship with secrets. "I don't blame Cecile for breaking up with me. She did the right thing for herself and, ultimately, for me too." He picked up a rock and threw it so far that a seagull changed its flight path when the rock splashed in the water. "Angry people and alcohol are an explosive combination, Maggie, and one night after Cecile dumped me, I was at the bar where I used to hang out. I don't remember what this one guy did that pissed me off so badly. It probably wasn't even that big a deal. But it was easy for me to go ballistic when I was in that frame of mind." Troy felt a chill flow through him as he recalled the strange way the memory of that night was stored in his mind. "I hit the guy so hard that he went down, hit his head on the sidewalk, and was immediately unconscious." He picked up another rock and bounced it nervously between his hands. "Maggie, I don't know what flash of awareness kicked in at that moment, but I will never forget the absolute worst feeling of dread and horror that I think I've ever felt in my life. I'm not sure how long it took, but until he finally opened his eyes, I thought I had killed him." He slowly wiped the sand from his hands. "That was the last time I've touched alcohol. I was so scared by the mixture of alcohol with my physical strength and anger that I made a vow to never drink again."

Maggie wasn't searching for shells any longer; she had her eyes on the wavy line between the ocean and the sky. When she turned to look at Troy, the tears that filled her eyes didn't quite spill into drops; they just shimmered in the light like pools of silver-green seawater. "Troy, I don't quite know what to say," she said.

Troy was relieved to hear her speak. He could feel his heart thumping in his chest; his fear was that she would think less of him, or even worse, find him impossible to love.

"I knew about Jason and Cecile, and I knew there had been some ugly times when you were in New Hampshire and that's why you came home. And I know you don't drink, which is something I actually admire." She wiped her eyes with the hem of the towel. "But it breaks my heart to think of the pain you were in." She smoothed an area of sand between her feet, drawing designs in the sand with her fingers and then wiping them away again. "Remember when we were up at Abe's after you helped him move all the stuff from the house where the old man died? You guys found all that money and gave it to Abe's friend, Rich—the guy with the charity for victims of violence."

"Yeah," he said.

"So, remember before you and Abe gave him the money, you went into Abe's office?"

"Yup."

"Well," Maggie said, "I didn't want to ask at the time because it seemed sorta between you two, but I remember that you guys came back into the room carrying that box of cash for Rich, and something seemed changed. Even though you never told me that story, you've mentioned things along the way that made me curious to know what that was about for you and Abe."

"What do you mean something seemed changed?" Now Troy was curious to understand what Maggie was able to perceive.

"Well, I remember you had been kind of quiet—not exactly moody—but really pensive that afternoon," Maggie explained. "And then after whatever you did with Abe, it was like something just changed. Like you seemed relieved or something."

Troy remembered the conversations he and Abe had while they drove to the job and spent the day working together. Abe told him that after he came back from Vietnam, he hadn't been able to leave the experience of war and violence behind. A random replay of uninvited memories kept his mind precariously balanced on a chronic edge of fear and rage. In the social climate of the late 1960s, Abe found his way to some Eastern philosophies, which then led him to the teachings of Buddhism. One of the many things Troy was relieved to learn from Abe was that yes, he could begin to rebuild his future into something very different from his past. He could soften the imprints of his past actions by carefully realigning his present thoughts, speech, and actions with intentions that were grounded in compassion.

"Well, yeah, I guess you're right," Troy agreed. Stacking small rocks into miniature towers, he clearly recalled what had taken place in those few minutes he and Abe spent preparing to present the money to Rich. "Abe brought that box out from his desk drawer and showed me the cash inside it." He remembered the way Abe looked at the photograph he kept on the wall of the friends he served with in Vietnam, most of whom were killed in the war. "Abe told me that he and I have some similar regrets. And that by setting a really special intention in our minds to ease the suffering not only for the people Rich helps, but for everyone everywhere, we could begin to convert those regrets into positive motivations. Those motivations eventually turn into actions that instead of bringing regret, bring good experiences." He reached for Maggie's hand. "I know it sounds weird, Mags, but when Abe said we should take a minute to just be quiet and reflect on all that before giving the money to Rich, I really did feel something change."

"Well then it wasn't just something in my imagination that I sensed. That sounds really powerful, but why didn't you tell me about it before?" Maggie asked.

"I wanted to tell you," he said. "But every time I thought about it, I knew I'd also have to tell you about the uglier things I did, and I chickened out." He took a rock from one of the towers he had built, and aiming for a buoy floating in the tide, he threw it within inches of his target. "I realized that if I'm holding back stuff that I think is important for you to know out of fear, then that's not about loving you. It's about cowardly protecting myself."

"That kind of honesty is huge, Troy," she said. "And yeah, I get it. I mean, I understand the fear, and I also understand the courage." Adding shells to the design she had just drawn into the sand, she reflected on his initial question. "And you're right. Even though none of this existed in my mind last year, I always hoped that I might meet someone like you." Patting the sand to frame her artwork, she added, "If it's possible, I think I love you even more now for your courage to share all this with me."

Another sense of relief washed over Troy as he experienced the truth in things Abe had taught him about peace of mind coming little-by-little when the things we do are motivated by loving kindness for someone besides just ourselves.

It wasn't much longer when the sun lowered behind some graying clouds and the breeze from the water grew cold.

"I'm freezing," Maggie said. "How about you? Are you ready to get going?"

"Sure, let's go," he agreed.

Maggie carefully folded her rocks and shells into her beach towel. They shook the sand from their blanket and walked barefoot back to the truck, leaving their stone towers and shell art behind.

⌣

Some, when they see their own blood,
Become especially brave and steady,
But some, when they see the blood of others,
Faint and fall unconscious.

These reactions come from the mind
Being either steady or timid.
Therefore, I should disregard harms caused to me,
And not be affected by suffering.

Even when the wise are suffering
Their minds remain very lucid and undefiled;
For when war is being waged against the disturbing
conceptions,
Much harm is caused at the time of battle.

The victorious warriors are those
Who, having disregarded all suffering,
Vanquish the foes of hatred and so forth;
(Common warriors) slay only corpses.
VI. 17, 18, 19, 20

The next morning, when Maggie heard Troy's truck skid into her driveway and the abrupt pull of the brakes, she knew that something was wrong. They were both scheduled for the breakfast shift, and Troy was picking her up for work. The smell of rain was in the air, and the truck's headlights shined misty beams of light across the gravel driveway. It was early, and her roommates were still sleeping. Maggie grabbed her

purse and keys and quietly pulled the door closed behind her.

She was barely in the truck when Troy said, "What
in God's name was my father thinking when he married that woman?"

Maggie couldn't tell if Troy was on the verge of
rage or of tears, but no matter what, she hated seeing
him hurt. "What happened?" she asked. "I thought
things were getting better between you two."

"Yeah, well… I thought so too." Troy's grip on the
steering wheel made the muscles in his forearms look
like one of DaVinci's drawings Maggie had been studying in art class. "But she freaked out on me again this
morning just as I was getting ready to leave," he said.

"What about?" Maggie asked. With the windows
rolled down, her hair blew across her face. She gathered it back and over to the side into a loose braid.

"What is it always about? Some ridiculous,
crazy-ass thing only she knows how to dream up."

"Well, did you *do* something or *say* something that
got her going?"

"You know what I did Maggie?" Even the muscles in his jaw were visible. "I was born, I exist, and
I happen to be one of my father's kids from his first
marriage." Here was the kernel of something that

never stopped hurting Troy, "It wasn't enough that she got my dad to leave my mom. Maureen wants to destroy any remnant that reminds her of the scumbag thing she did." He took a breath while he waited to turn at the intersection. "And my dad doesn't have the balls to stand up to her because he knows none of it would have happened if he hadn't signed up for the ride."

"Okay." Maggie wanted to understand what happened, but she realized it might take awhile before Troy got around to telling her. "Well, we all know Maureen's a piece of work, and her little world of decorator magazines doesn't allow for things like stepchildren. I guess you just remind her that her dream world isn't based on reality, and she really just doesn't cope well with that."

One of the many things Troy appreciated about Maggie was her knack for summing things up. Feeling understood was like releasing a little air from an over-inflated tire. He started to let the anger dissipate. "You know what I did, Maggie?"

"No. What?" she asked.

"I put a fricking coffee mug in the bottom rack of the dishwasher instead of in the top rack." He laughed at the absurdity of his transgression.

"Seriously?" Maggie had expected something more offensive.

"Yup." He grew quiet. "I know she's just out of her mind and I shouldn't take it personally, and I know better than to let it get to me, but sometimes everything I know gets short-circuited or something, and I start feeling every bit as crazy as she is." He drummed his fingers on the steering wheel while he collected his thoughts. "At least I didn't yell back at her, but I slammed the door so hard, I heard something fall in the kitchen when I left."

"If all you did was slam the door, I'd say you did pretty well." Maggie's sincerity was comforting.

"Yeah, I guess it could've been worse. But, Maggie, after everything I learned from Grace and Abe, I know there's another way to respond." Troy hated carrying regrets and had been making an effort not to accumulate new ones. Anger, since it precipitates so much that is destructive, was high on his list of things to reduce precisely for that reason.

"For God's sake, Troy, you're human—you're going to get angry sometimes," Maggie said. "I know Grace and Abe are both amazing people, but even they've got feet of clay." She rubbed his shoulder reassuringly. "Lighten up."

"Feet of clay?" Troy asked. "What does that mean?"

"Oh, it's something my grandmother used to say. I think it comes from the Bible," Maggie explained. "Even though someone might appear to be better than most, they're still vulnerable to the same flaws as the rest of us."

"You're right." Troy felt his anger soften as his emotions began to register the wisdom of reason. He couldn't undo his stormy reaction, but he could make an effort to make up for it in some way. It didn't matter so much if she was right or wrong. He had learned that Maureen, and everyone else to varying degrees, is suffering from an ignorance that infuses the mind with something quite toxic. Grace had taught him about the Three Poisons: anger, ignorance, and desire. She explained that all three cause people to do things that bring harm to others while they additionally bring more harm upon themselves. Both Grace and Abe explained that when we don't recognize that everything exists interdependently, our thinking and therefore our behavior becomes skewed and brings unpleasant results. Grace took it a step further by talking about past lives and future lives. Grace told him that Buddhists believe that throughout countless eons, all beings have at one time been everyone's precious mother. So even the person who most annoys you, and for whom you feel nothing but disgust, has at one time been someone who took care of you and sacrificed her own happiness for yours—just like a very kind mother. The purpose of thinking like this, she explained, is to recall their kindness and generate the wish to repay it. Even though he wasn't sold on multiple lifetimes or that maybe the hawk circling his backyard had once been his mother, he was willing to try it out as an exercise. Troy found that this really did help him feel a surprisingly deep compassion for Maureen. The compassion he felt was so strong that the next time she laced into him, his compassion didn't dissipate. In fact, it grew stronger. He was amazed by how powerfully things changed in that compassionate moment and that Maureen actually offered a tearful apology. Like anything, it would require consistent practice in order to make a more lasting imprint. This morning's episode with Maureen reminded him that he still had a long way to go.

Troy and Maggie pulled into the parking lot behind the diner with only a few minutes to spare before work. As Troy parked the truck, a few raindrops fell just before the sky opened into a loud, heavy rain.

"Uh-oh. Ready to run, Maggie? Or do you want me to drop you at the door?" Troy asked.

"Let's run. It'll feel good." Laughing, she pulled up the hood of her sweatshirt and ran with Troy across the parking lot and in through the back door to the diner.

⌣

As I do not become angry
With great sources of suffering such as jaundice,
Then why be angry with animate creatures?
They, too, are provoked by conditions.

Although they are not wished for,
These sicknesses arise;
And likewise, although they are not wished for,
These disturbing conceptions forcibly arise.

Without thinking, "I shall be angry,"
People become angry with no resistance,
And without thinking, "I shall produce myself,"
Likewise anger itself is produced.
VI. 22, 23, 24

Soon the coffee makers began to hiss and steam as they filled a row of pots with decaf and regular. Troy enjoyed the way the smell of coffee permeated the air on rainy days as if the air itself became caffeinated. The rain poured so hard that through the steam-fogged windows the street outside looked like a river of sliding asphalt. Tables were being set, bread made ready for toasting, and pitchers filled with ice water when the first few customers came through the door, closing their dripping umbrellas and leaning them against the front wall.

These were the customers Troy considered to be the die-hard crew that came early each morning on their way to work. Typically they took seats at the counter where they began their day in friendly, light-hearted company. Troy thought that maybe happiness is a contagious thing when he realized he was already feeling better than when he left his house just a short while earlier. He had worked at the diner long enough that many of the customers knew him by name. They would ask him how he was doing in that casual way that doesn't really listen for the answer but assumes everything's good. The rain hadn't been a deterrent for the tables to fill, and it wasn't long before the morning rhythm was in full swing.

Once inside, people seemed less inclined to rush than on other days, so while new arrivals slowed, the diner remained full of people staying for pastries and additional cups of coffee. Checking their watches and texting messages to offices or appointments, they eventually emptied their coffee cups and pushed off into the day.

By ten-thirty, the downpour slowed to a light drizzle before the sun took over. Wet green leaves, blades of grass, and store windows burst sunlight into the world. Maggie opened the door and stepped onto the sidewalk, checking the sky for rainbows. Coming up empty, she turned to go back inside when she recognized Mrs. Sternau walking toward her. Even with a cane, she moved gracefully, and her white hair shined like sunlight itself.

"Good morning, Mrs. Sternau," Maggie greeted her. "It's not Thursday; I'm surprised to see you here this morning."

"Good morning, dear," Mrs Sternau answered. "My goodness, I hope I'm not such a creature of habit that I can't break from tradition now and then. Besides, I am having a strong yen for pancakes that can't wait until next week."

"Oh, I see." Maggie held the door for her. "Well, come on in, it looks like your table is waiting for you."

"Thank you, dear." The quintessential New Englander of an earlier era, Mrs. Sternau's manner of speech and movements were impeccably proper. Maggie was intrigued by her demeanor and noticed that she herself reflexively added an extra layer of politeness to her own behavior.

"Would you like decaf or regular coffee this morning, Mrs. Sternau?" Maggie asked, carrying a pot of each in her hands.

"Regular would be lovely. Thank you."

"Can I get you anything else besides pancakes?" Maggie asked while she filled Mrs. Sternau's coffee cup.

Unfolding her napkin and smoothing it on her lap, she answered, "If you have melons, I would love to have a small slice with lemon."

"Yes, we do have melons," Maggie said. "I'll get some for you."

"Oh, delightful. Thank you." Sitting in the sunlight with her coffee, Mrs. Sternau was a picture of contentment.

"Look who's here," Maggie whispered to Troy as she passed him on her way into the kitchen. "She had a *yen* for pancakes and melons," she told him, amused by the way Mrs. Sternau expressed it.

He glanced over at the seat by the window and smiled. "Then it's a damn good thing it stopped raining. We wouldn't want anything to stand in the way of Mrs. Sternau and pancakes."

There was another table to clear and reset near where Mrs. Sternau was sitting, so Troy used the opportunity to walk in her direction.

"Good morning, Mrs. Sternau." With nothing else that came to mind, Troy thought weather was a good way to open a conversation. "That was quite a rain this morning, wasn't it?"

"Oh my gracious, yes," she agreed. "My gutters are so full it looked like waterfalls were pouring from my house."

"It sounds like you need to have your gutters cleaned," Troy said. "I have a ladder and a truck. I'd be happy to take care of them for you."

"Do you have time for a job like that?" she asked before adding hopefully, "I live in a very small house."

"Yes, of course. But we'll need to wait a few days for all those leaves to dry out after the rain." He took a napkin from another table setting. "If you give me your phone number, I can call you in a few days, and we'll set something up." He went to the cashier's counter to find a pen and brought it back to Mrs. Sternau.

"Very well, then. If you are sure it won't be too much trouble." She wrote her phone number on the napkin. "And here is my address."

Troy looked at the address. "Oh, I think I know where this is. Is your house in the neighborhood near the woods by the pond?"

"Yes, it is," she answered. "My husband and I moved there nearly sixty years ago."

Maggie came to the table carrying a plate with melon and a wedge of lemon and placed it in front of Mrs. Sternau. "Your pancakes will be coming soon."

"This looks delicious. Thank you."

"Well, enjoy your breakfast, Mrs. Sternau." Troy picked up the bus pan to clear the other table.

With things slowing down, Troy found himself revisiting the angry exchange with Maureen. Several months earlier Grace had explained that when someone carries on the way Maureen does, they are suffering similarly to someone with a physical illness. Just as you would feel compassion for anyone in physical pain, it is entirely logical and appropriate to feel compassion for someone like Maureen. She told him that by not understanding how they and all things truly exist, people mistakenly operate from a mind that views themselves and others as if they exist completely separately and self sufficiently. This view is known as ignorance, and it distorts the way people perceive things. For instance they mistakenly classify others in categories either of an enemy, a friend, or a neutral person if there's no feeling of closeness or dislike at all. Putting those misleading classifications into the context of the cause and effect nature of reality, Troy thought it all worked like falling dominoes. If he didn't have the karma to meet certain conditions in the first place, then meeting a challenging person such as Maureen wouldn't happen. And if it were all about Maureen being an inherently difficult person, then his father wouldn't feel she was so very lovable. So if she's not inherently obnoxious, then she's not inherently wonderful or inherently anything. However, with the participation of his own karma and perception, things have the illusion of being inherently existent. Adding another twist to it all, since change is constant, friends can become enemies, and enemies can become friends. Troy understood that negative actions, especially those driven by anger and hatred, leave only destruction in their wake. The falling dominoes become the wake that churns the waters that the angry person, without fail, will have to navigate in the future.

These things all made sense when Grace had talked about them. But as he imagined himself back in his earlier scene with Maureen, there was a more dominant inner voice that began defiantly reminding him that Maureen is out of her mind, and that he was perfectly entitled to be outraged and should have flipped out right back at her. He began thinking of all the things he could have said and maybe should have said. While he was wiping down tables and adding fresh place settings, his mind, armed with an uncensored vocabulary, raced with possible ways he might have verbally ripped her to shreds. Imagining this scene filled him with an energy that felt righteous, powerful, and destructive. His mind felt quickly at home in the old habitual groove of well-rehearsed ignorance that rejected the understanding and perspective Grace had taught him. As he placed forks, knives, and spoons neatly on the table, his eyes were no longer seeing the place settings. They were watching the unfolding of the imaginary showdown with Maureen and with himself as the victor triumphantly cutting her down to size.

"Excuse me, Trevor," Mrs. Sternau's voice interrupted his mental tirade.

He shook the angry scene from his mind and felt something like the grateful relief that comes when you open your eyes from a bad dream and realize you had only been dreaming. He walked to Mrs. Sternau's table. "Yes?" he asked, clearing his throat. "Can I get you something?"

A good reminder, he thought. *This is exactly what Grace was talking about. Why wouldn't I feel the same kindness and willingness to help Maureen as I do for Mrs. Sternau? It's my perception of considering one an enemy and the other a friend that makes me want to rip Maureen apart and help Mrs. Sternau.*

"I would love a splash more coffee, but I don't see Molly." Her voice drew Troy away from his own thoughts. "Would you please let her know?" Her brown eyes had the ring of blue around the irises that often happens to people as they age. "I will have decaf this time."

"I'll get the coffee for you," Troy said as he took the plate with the melon rind and collapsed lemon wedge. "Are you still working on the pancakes?"

"Yes I am, dear. They are absolutely heavenly," she said, holding her fork curved side down in her left hand and knife in her right, positioned like hands of a clock at eight-twenty. "Of course the maple syrup you serve here is the pure syrup, which makes all the difference in the world for pancakes." Her smile gave a glimpse into her young spirit that appeared to be alive and well.

"I couldn't agree with you more," Troy said.

Mrs. Sternau finished her pancakes, swirling the last few pieces in the extra syrup she had poured on her plate. While she waited for her check she sipped her second cup of coffee and wrote another message on her placemat before she and her cane were on their way.

Dearest,

The paperboy delivered this morning's news. It was another onslaught of fear and hatred. How I wish you were here, teaching students that there is no wisdom in anger or true benefit in its result. As you and I learned all those years ago, anger merely reveals the great need for loving kindness and patience.

Adoringly,
Esther

"How did she know, or *did* she even know and this is just a weird coincidence?" Troy asked after he showed the note to Maggie. Troy told her that he had been getting himself all worked up again about Maureen until Mrs. Sternau asked for more coffee. "And then when I read her note, it felt like she must've read my mind or something."

They had finished work and were getting ready to leave. Maggie took her purse and sweatshirt from the closet near the kitchen.

"I don't know, Troy. But I also don't know if it really matters." She continued toward the door. "I guess what matters is what you take from it. I mean, when I read her notes, I think she's just continuing to do what she always did when her husband was alive—sharing life with him. Sometimes that could be little things like stuff about the garden, and sometimes it could be weightier things like what's going on in the world."

"I guess you're right," Troy said. He wasn't going to say more, but on another level, he didn't entirely agree. Maggie's explanation didn't satisfy the question of how Mrs. Sternau's letters often had a quality of being perfectly tailored to something Troy had been dealing with or even just mulling over. Besides, Maggie hadn't been with him the day Abe talked about things that happened in Vietnam and that eventually led him to study and practice Buddhist teachings. In particular, he was reminded about something Abe had said over lunch about karma and the uncanny things that began happening as his practice in mindfulness deepened. He told Troy that several things go on with mindfulness practice when it's taken beyond a sitting-in-meditation kind of mindfulness. The vigilant mindfulness Abe had talked about of thoughts, speech, motivations, and actual actions taken are things we don't think about very often unless someone brings it to our attention the way Abe had for Troy. Abe said that when you learn to bring your own attention to mindfulness, it's like everything gets another kind of spin to it. He said that karmic seeds are ripening all the time, and once you begin this practice and experience enough fluky or coincidental things, you begin to realize it's really neither fluky nor coincidental, but the logical unfolding of your own karma. And once you truly understand that, there is no way you want to generate anything but positive karma. But he wasn't going to explain all this to Maggie now. It wasn't yet firm enough in his own mind.

"When you go to clean her gutters, I want to go with you." Maggie said. "I'll hold the ladder for you so you won't fall, okay?"

"I won't fall, but thanks, Mags."

⌒

My mind will not experience peace
If it fosters painful thoughts of hatred.
I shall find no joy or happiness;
Unable to sleep, I shall feel unsettled.
VI. 3

It was arranged that a week from Tuesday Troy would borrow his father's ladder and tarp and be at Mrs. Sternau's in the morning. Maggie was behind on a project due for art class and wasn't able to join him.

For the moment, things were smoothed over with Maureen. Troy apologized for slamming the door and said he hoped nothing had broken. Maureen didn't exactly apologize for her own behavior, but coming from Maureen, what she did say came close. She explained that she had been unable to sleep, which was why she had been up so early unloading the dishwasher as he was getting ready to leave. She told him that she had been irritable about something else and the timing was just unfortunate and she simply lost her temper. This is the nature of anger. Among other things, it interferes with sleep and short circuits a peaceful mind into one that is erratic and destructive. Troy thought her reasoning validated what Grace explained to be why anger is considered one of the Three Poisons. And with that understanding in mind, it also validated why compassion is the only reasonable response. He too had unleashed an irrational temper on others in the past and could consider encounters with Maureen's anger to be the natural ripening of the karmic seeds he himself had planted.

The neighborhood where Mrs. Sternau lived was familiar to Troy. When he was younger, he and his friends played hockey on the pond in the woods when the ice was frozen thick and solid. Back when his parents were still married, the whole family took sleds and toboggans into the woods where there was a long hill for sledding. He could still remember piling onto the toboggan, sandwiched between his brothers, and the thrill of sliding down the hill, gaining speed when their father gave them a push. But strangely, he couldn't remember his mother and father together even though he knew they had both been there. Sometimes he would strain to remember what it was like when his parents were married. Other than some photographs in an album his mother kept, he couldn't bring the memory to life no matter how hard he tried.

The road came to an end where a long stonewall marked the border between the woods and the properties on either side of the road. On the left was Mrs. Sternau's house, just as she had described—a small white clapboard cottage with a perennial garden in the front yard that was blooming irises, poppies, bluebells, and other flowers Troy didn't know the names of. Troy backed his truck into the driveway and walked on the stone pathway under the rose trellis to Mrs. Sternau's front door. He heard classical music coming from inside the house, and the door was open with only the narrow frame of the screen door to knock on.

"Hello?" He waited. "Mrs. Sternau?"

"Yes, Trevor, I'll be right there."

He laughed a little to himself about how absolutely certain she was that his name was Trevor. He didn't have the heart to risk confusing her by correcting her.

"Please come in," Mrs. Sternau said as she turned the tarnished brass handle on the screen door to open it.

"Thank you." Troy wiped his sneakers on the mat outside before stepping into a small foyer and into the home that held the history and the muse for Mrs. Sternau's notes. The floors were dark wood, and the lemon-yellow walls were lined with large oil paintings in ornate frames. Shelves built into an entire wall were packed tightly with books. One large book, titled *Masters of the Mahamudra*, was placed on its side like a bookend to the others. On the oval coffee table was a newspaper opened to the crossword puzzle, a pencil, dictionary, magnifying glass, and a china cup sitting in its saucer with a sip or two of coffee remaining.

"Can I get you something to drink?" Mrs. Sternau asked. "I can offer you either lemonade or ginger ale."

"Not now, thank you," he said. "But maybe after I've taken care of the gutters."

"You are so kind to come help me," Mrs. Sternau said. "Please follow me. I'll take you out back through the porch."

Troy followed her onto the porch where white metal patio furniture with vinyl cushions of yellow and green floral designs was arranged the way it might have been for decades. He pictured Mrs. Sternau and her husband spending summer evenings in this room. Glasses of wine would sit on coasters while they cut pieces of cheese with wooden-handled knives and ate cheese with crackers held over small square cocktail napkins. And when it grew dark enough, fireflies ignited sparks of light from the woods, while Beethoven played softly in the next room. If he had grandparents to visit, he would have liked to visit them here. They would have seen to it that he was loved in that wonderful way grandparents patiently love and understand children and teach them the world can be a kind place.

"Here is where all the trouble was brewing in the downpour last week," Mrs. Sternau said as she walked carefully with her cane down the stone step from the porch onto the terrace. "If the wind had come from another direction, the floor would have been drenched."

"I'll take care of that for you. It won't take me long." Troy evaluated the height of the gutters. Except for possibly a few spots, the stepladder he brought with him would be tall enough. He might need the extension ladder to work around the large rhododendron and some of the other shrubs. "I'll go get the ladder and tarp from my truck and get started."

"Is there anything I can do to help?" she asked with full-hearted sincerity.

"Thank you, but I think I've got it covered," he said. "Please do whatever you were doing when I got here. I noticed the crossword puzzle on your table. Maybe you can finish it by the time I finish the gutters."

"Very well, then. Please call me if you need anything," she said.

A pair of work gloves hanging from his back pocket, Troy carried the ladder across the lawn and set it up outside the porch. He spread the tarp on the ground before he put on the gloves and climbed the ladder. The soggier leaves at the bottom of the gutters landed with a muted thump when he dropped them by handfuls onto the tarp. Moving the ladder a few feet at a time, he worked his way from one side of the house to the next. When the tarp was loaded with leaves, he pulled the corners together and carried it over his shoulder like a sack to the edge of the property and dumped the leaves into the woods beyond the stonewall. A wooden bench under a pair of beech trees looked as if it hadn't been visited in ages. Its white paint was stained by rain and wind-splashed dirt, and at least a season or two of beech seedpods collected in its corners.

For no particular reason other than some pull of gravity, Troy left the empty tarp by the wall and walked over the mossy part of the lawn to sit on the bench. From that seat he could view the house and the garden—the gardens within gardens that Mrs. Sternau wrote about in some of her notes—beds of tiger lilies and day lilies, and a walkway lined by delicate wild rose bushes, lily of the valley, and sweet woodruff. Troy considered this bench might be where Professor Sternau would come to enjoy his work, like a painter standing back from his easel after an afternoon of painting. There was a sense of peace that arose from this view of the garden. So much so that Troy thought it could only have been created by someone who himself carried that feeling of peace within as he cared for it.

He rested for just a few minutes before he took himself from his contemplation, stood and picked up the tarp, folded it loosely under his arms, and carried it back to the truck. He then put the ladder away, slapped the dirt from his jeans and hands, and walked back inside through the porch door.

"Mrs. Sternau?" he called out before he entered. "The gutters are done."

"Already?" Mrs. Sternau came out from the kitchen. Troy noticed that she didn't have her cane, but he could see it hanging close by from the counter's edge in the small kitchen. "Please come and sit down. I've made egg salad sandwiches. You must have an appetite by now."

"Thank you. But where can I wash my hands?" Troy asked.

"Oh yes, of course," she said. "The powder room is just down the hall to the right."

All mistakes that occur
And all the various kinds of wrongdoing
Arise through the force of conditions;
They do not govern themselves.

These conditions that assemble together
Have no intention to produce anything,
And neither does their product
Have the intention to be produced.
VI. 25, 26

Mrs. Sternau had set the table for two. "Please have a seat," she said.

A sandwich overflowing with egg salad and lettuce on rye bread, a scoop of potato salad, and two slices of pickles were arranged on a blue and gold-rimmed plate. A large glass mug filled with lemonade, silverware, and a cloth napkin were set in traditional symmetry on a dark blue placemat.

"Thank you." Feeling somewhat awkward in their role reversal, Troy took his seat.

Mrs. Sternau sat opposite Troy. On her plate was a sandwich, a smaller portion of potato salad, and one slice of pickle. She bowed her head slightly and sat quietly for a moment before lifting her fork.

"You know, Trevor," she began. "It *is* Trevor, isn't it?"

Troy cleared his throat. He felt apologetic but couldn't lie. "Um, no. It's Troy."

"Oh for goodness sakes," she said. "I have such difficulty keeping things straight. Oh well, it's one of those things that happens as we age." She used her fork and knife to cut the pickle into bite-sized pieces while she talked. "Well, *Troy*," she said, emphasizing his name. "I am so grateful to you for taking care of the gutters for me. It must be years since they were last cleaned. There are so many things to keep track of in caring for this house, and since my husband, may he rest in peace, passed away, I'm afraid the gutters are one of those things that slip my mind."

"No problem, Mrs. Sternau. I'm happy to help." Having seen Mrs. Sternau use a fork and knife for her pickle, Troy thought he ought to do the same. His friends would die laughing if they saw him. "I enjoy working outside, especially in nice weather like to-day. It's a good break from school work and bussing tables."

"Oh, you're a student?" Her face lit up. "Are you studying at the university?"

"No, I'm not." He didn't want to confess the long version of his education woes. "I'm taking night class-es at the community college."

"Lovely," she said. "I wish you might have known my husband, Albert. He was a professor, you know."

"I wish I could have known him too." In truth, he felt they had already met through the notes she left at the diner.

As if something had distracted her, or in some way taken her attention, she looked beyond Troy into the next room—the room where she had been working on the crossword puzzle. Her voice took a more distant tone. "Oh yes," she said. "Yes, I must." Then, her voice resumed its previous tone when she brought her attention back to Troy.

"When young people see old people, they tend to simply see them as old. They can't see the history that inched them, day-by-day, into their wrinkled skin and stiffened backs." She set her fork and knife down on her plate. "Something has come to mind with an urgency that tells me I must share it with you. And, when things come to my mind in a strong way such as this, I don't waste time or ignore them for fear I'll forget if I wait too long."

Troy saw her look into the next room again, and this time he turned to look too. He saw only the bookshelves, the curved wooden back of the Victorian style loveseat, the view of the garden through the windows, and a table with a photograph in a frame.

"You have a history too, and even though you have no wrinkles to show for it, I feel you have been blessed in the way of the double-edged sword. In other words, there has been a great deal of pain, but you benefit from that pain by developing wisdom." She closed her eyes while she recited, "May I view one whom I greatly hoped would help me, but instead mistreats or even harms me as my greatest spiritual teacher."[1] She opened her eyes and softly smiled.

Troy just listened, forcing himself to hold his focus on what she was saying and not the questions that began to form in his mind—like who was she talking to in the next room?

---

1   *The Essence of Mahayana Lojong Practice: A Commentary to Geshe Langri Tangpa's Mind Training in Eight Verses* by Sermey Khensur Lobsang Tharchin, Verse VI

But what if someone should obstruct
my gaining merit?
With them, too, it is incorrect to be angry;
For since there is no fortitude similar to patience,
Surely I should put it into practice.

If due to my own failings,
I am not patient with this (enemy),
Then it is only I who am preventing myself
From practicing this cause for gaining merit.

If without it, something does not occur,
And if with it, it does come to be,
Then since this (enemy) would be
the cause of (patience)
How can I say that (the enemy) prevents it?
VI. 102, 103, 104

"Albert and I learned to keep a peaceful mind at a time when others took steps to harm us. Albert was a history professor, and a darned good one. I've never known anyone more eager to get up and out the door to work than Albert. I believe he loved teaching history so much because he cared so deeply about young people and for their potental to build a better future. He knew the young students he taught were maturing into the designers of the future. Inspired by Gandhi's life, and moved by the tragedy of his assassination in 1948, Albert devoted several courses to non-violence and to the powerful influence of Gandhi's life and work in the world.

"It is all so long ago now. Many people today may not remember that the 1950s were tense with a certain kind of fear. People were extremely anxious about the spread of communism. Here in our country, the war in Korea wasn't going well, and the communist advances in Eastern Europe and in China were of grave concern. Efforts were made to make sure communism couldn't spread, and so the entire country was primed and instructed to be on the lookout for the enemy of communism infiltrating our society. Then along came Senator Joseph McCarthy. McCarthy was a politician who craved power, fame, and attention and realized he could have it all by riding this wave of fear and by filling people with more fear. Through any stretch of association, he and his committee, supported by a reckless and irresponsible press, came up with a list of individuals they accused of being either communist or communist sympathizers. McCarthy's influence was immense, and the people on his list were subjected to viciously destructive and aggressive investigations. He and his committee went after government employees, people in the entertainment industry, writers, educators, artists, intellectuals, union activists, and more. People lost their jobs, careers were destroyed, and some people were imprisoned. As things turned out, most everything that took place during that time was declared unconstitutional, and punishments that had come about through trial verdicts were eventually overturned. But some people were never able to rebuild their careers, even years later.

"But why am I telling you all this? Well, let me back up a little. A friend of Albert's from his own college days was applying for a job and asked Albert if he would write a letter of recommendation. Of course Albert was happy to write the recommendation. But when his friend's name came up on one of McCarthy's lists, it was through this connection that Albert's name was then listed as a communist sympathizer too. Even though the charges were unfounded and nothing was proven, the university told Albert he must resign from his position. They had received notice that he was to be subpoenaed for a court hearing and couldn't risk the university's reputation by even the slightest scent of association with investigations of this magnitude. I will never forget my husband's despair and outrage when we understood that not only was he out of a job, but the career he loved and had planned to devote his life to could be destroyed.

"As you might imagine, it was a very dark time. Most people, lawyers included, were too frightened to help anyone like Albert who was tangled up in this issue for fear they too might be blacklisted. But my husband was a very courageous and very wise man. After the initial shock, Albert thought of Gandhi's example and made a commitment that he would not let anger and hatred consume him, and he would somehow find a way—a peaceful way—to continue his life's work. But he knew this would not be an easy commitment to keep. He would need more strength than he was confident he had in order to move forward and to not let this experience destroy him.

"Until we could get back on our feet, our very dear family friends, the Lanimakers, invited us to stay with them while we sorted through all that had happened. That was when we left Maryland and came north." Pausing, Mrs. Sternau took a bite of her sandwich—a sandwich that she ate not with her hands but with a knife and fork as if it were the most normal thing in the world. "I was happy to come here," she said, "because even though my own parents were no longer living, this is where I grew up and where I always felt a sense of home."

"I've heard about McCarthyism," Troy said. "And now I'm beginning to wish I'd paid more attention during history class. I've never known anyone whose life was directly affected like yours. And you're right, it's probably not something people think much about these days."

"Well, it wouldn't hurt for people to remember the lessons learned. I'll leave it at that, because more importantly there are other things we need to talk about."

What did she mean, *things we need to talk about*? Where was this all coming from? Again, Troy looked into the other room, trying to spot what she was looking at when she interrupted herself again.

"I know, I know. I'm getting there," she whispered as if she didn't realize Troy could hear her.

"Who are you talking to?" he asked.

Surprised by his question, "Why, you of course," she answered.

By it, friends and relatives are disheartened;
Though drawn by my generosity, they will not trust me;
In brief, there is nobody
Who lives happily with anger.

Hence the enemy, anger,
Creates sufferings such as these,
But whoever assiduously overcomes it
Finds happiness now and hereafter.

Having found its fuel of mental unhappiness
In the prevention of what I wish for,
And in doing what I do not want,
Hatred increases and then destroys me.

Therefore, I should totally eradicate
The fuel of this enemy;
For this enemy has no other function
Than that of causing me harm.
VI. 5,6,7,8

"Ruth Lanimaker's father was a geologist. His work had been in Java where Ruth and her brother were born and raised in the 1920s. Their mother had a very strong spirit that helped her make the most of what others might have considered a difficult lifestyle. Living so far from the rest of her family back in the States was very different then from how it would be today. For instance, one couldn't make intercontinental phone calls, and letters sent home were carried on a six-week voyage by ship. That meant if Ruth's mother asked a simple question in a letter, even if the person responded right away, it would be three months before she would receive an answer. Travel over oceans was only by ship at that time and, since it was quite a long journey home, visiting family and friends only happened a handful of times.

"Ruth's mother made sure the family took advantage of sampling interesting things the island and its culture had to offer. Ruth told me stories about attending a sultan's wedding, a trip to see a volcano by horseback at dawn, and several visits to the famous Buddhist temple Borobudur. When her mother first visited the temple, she was so moved by an extraordinary feeling of peace that she grew fascinated to know the history of the temple. A guide at the temple explained the stages of mental preparation for enlightenment that were shown in the relief panels that wound their way in ascending rectangular pathways through the levels of Borobudur. The lower level panels illustrate the pitfalls of the realm of desire where things like desire, hatred, and ignorance drive beings further into suffering. Then, as one continues higher, the panels depict how one can conquer these and other afflictions until the pathways eventually arrive into a round summit where the meditating Buddhas sit in supreme bliss. In the center, a bell-shaped tower points to the blissful realm known as Nirvana. Listening to the guide's explanation, she became absorbed by a desire to know more. Ruth showed us her mother's photograph albums from her very unusual childhood. Even when seen in black and white, Borobudur and its surroundings are truly breathtaking.

"Have you ever noticed when your mind becomes genuinely fascinated by something that it points like a compass needle strongly attracted to due north? And the very things you long to know more about find a way of making appearances in your life? Sometimes it happens through random conversation, or you might just pick up a magazine with an article that gives you just the right insight into something you wished to understand."

Troy thought of the book on Grace's bookshelf he gravitated to simply because its cover reminded him of things he had enjoyed learning in Asian Studies class. When he began reading the book, his interest grew and it was like riding a wave that led to deeper conversations with Grace and then to meeting Abe. Clearly, he thought, he must still be riding that wave.

"Yeah, come to think of it, I have noticed that," he said.

"Well, that's the way it went for Mrs. Berridger, Ruth's dear mother. Since the influence of Buddhism in Java had waned long since the time Borobudur was built, resources for learning were few." Covering her mouth politely, she laughed, "But I've lived long enough to know that with a sincere motivation, once certain wheels are set in motion, there is just no stopping their progress.

"One evening the Berridgers had been socializing with some expat friends as they often did. This particular evening it was over a game of Bridge when Mrs. Berridger talked about her visits to Borobudur. Since it was a fairly popular site, some of the other guests had visited the temple too. One of the guests especially appreciated Mrs. Berridger's desire to know more about Buddhist philosophy and view of life. He told her that living on the edge of town was a man who devoted his life to the study and practice of Buddhism. He had returned from many years in Tibet where he traveled in search of the teachings of those who had built Borobudur. Since his return to Java, he was teaching a small but growing group of students. Mrs. Berridger asked the man to please take her and her husband to meet the teacher. Mr. Berridger didn't have nearly the enthusiasm that Mrs. Berridger had, but he felt it only

fair that he support her interest since she was so toler-
ant of the lifestyle his career imposed on their family.

"After meeting him, she learned that when the
teacher was a young man he'd left Java for Tibet to
study in a Buddhist monastery. The monastery's lineage
came from a highly regarded teacher named Atisha.
Over a thousand years earlier, Atisha traveled from
India to Sumatra, a neighboring island to Java. After
twelve years in Sumatra, Atisha returned to India and
then later went to Tibet. It was the new teacher's wish
that the pure teachings be brought back to his home-
land. So he welcomed all students, even westerners and
even women, which in those days wasn't always a given.
Ruth's mother became one of his most dedicated students. Her father's work was his main occupation, so he
didn't study along with his wife. But Ruth said she remembered that her father enjoyed hearing second-hand
about the things his wife learned. In their later years,
when reminiscing about that time in their lives, he com-
mented that he couldn't help but notice the happiness it
brought to his wife and therefore to their family.

"In addition to overseeing her children's education
in math, science, and literature, Ruth's mother also
shared things she was learning about Buddhist teachings. And as Ruth and her brother grew older, they

studied directly with their mother's teacher. Whenever Ruth spoke of her family's teacher, her entire being seemed to smile like someone newly in love. I never met him of course, but it was impossible to miss that he was quite extraordinary.

"But back to Ruth's mother. By applying the teachings in her own life and understanding the nature of karma, feelings of homesickness and resentment over being separated from the rest of her family were softened. She rejoiced in the rare opportunity to study the dharma in a country where it was available—although certainly not in the large scale of its earlier history. If there is truth to the apple not falling far from the tree, Ruth's compassionate, joyful, and generous nature must have had its roots in her unique upbringing."

"That's amazing," Troy interrupted. "I've been learning a lot about karma lately."

"Yes, I know," she said as if he had merely announced something like *the sky is blue* and continued telling her story.

"When Albert and I were welcomed into Ruth and Harold's home, we found a perfect refuge from the tumultuous ordeal we had been in the throes of. You see, while we had left the scene of the crime so to speak, the experience wasn't exactly behind us. We still had to forge and travel an uncertain road in order to rebuild our lives. And the dark clouds of anger that periodically grew quite stormy were our biggest hindrance. Frankly, everyone's life is an uncertain road ahead, and what we do with our mind and emotions will determine how well we deal with that uncertainty. But that topic might best be saved for later.

"Even though Albert was committed to his Gandhi-inspired ideals, there were great and what seemed to be insurmountable challenges. As I said, there were times when deep anger would rise up, and poor Albert felt absolutely destroyed. He missed his students, he missed teaching, he missed waking up happy to be going to work, and, when he wasn't too angry, he missed his fellow professors.

"Ruth and I had often talked about Buddhism over the years. I was eager to learn more, but, as was the case for Ruth's mother, the teachings weren't commonly available in this country. I heard that Henry David Thoreau and Ralph Waldo Emerson had been influenced by Buddhist philosophy, so I knew reference books must be available if only I looked hard enough. But with Ruth as my very close friend, I had an excellent teacher. Ruth gave Albert and me instruction on specific teachings and practices that helped to change everything from that point on. So, you see, I must share what we learned with you.

"Because it strikes against the root of suffering, Ruth told us that there is no instruction more important than the teaching of patience. She began by explaining that it is the nature of things to disappoint us. It is the nature of possessions to be lost. And it is the nature of things to deteriorate. 'Open your eyes to the world,' Ruth said, 'and know that it cannot possibly give you lasting satisfaction.' Albert and I were experiencing the world in such a way that it was easy to accept that statement. She taught us to understand that both happiness and unhappiness merely arise from the mind. There is nothing that arises from only nothing, and therefore everything exists in dependence upon causes and conditions. Knowing that happiness and unhappiness arise from the mind, if we train our minds to be always mindful of the interdependent nature of all that exists, we can then learn to eliminate the causes of anger. Can you imagine the potential for peace in the world if people learned to eliminate the causes of anger, and truly understood it was within their control to do so?"

"If everyone could really see the logic in what you're saying, then yes," Troy answered. "I think most people feel there are so many bad things going on in the world that the only reasonable response *is* anger. If you're not angry, then they think something's wrong with you."

"Well then, to get started let us look at the reasons one gets angry. When anger comes in defense of ourselves or on behalf of people we care about, it is for these reasons." Mrs. Sternau pressed on a different finger for each reason she counted. "When a circumstance brings physical or emotional pain and suffering to ourselves or to people we like, when we or people we care about have been treated disrespectfully, when someone verbally attacks us or attacks someone we care about, and when someone says something unkind about us or about our friends. Oh my, Albert and I were quite familiar with that one. When one's reputation is tarnished, it is extremely disturbing to the mind.

"But here is an interesting other side of the coin that switches all those reasons for anger upside down. When these exact same things come to people we do *not* like or to whom we consider to be an enemy, we have an entirely different set of responses. We get angry when things go well for people we don't like, we are happy when they are disrespected, we gloat when someone attacks our enemies verbally, and we are happy when others say unkind things about them to destroy their reputation.

"Why should identical actions bring about entirely different reactions for one group of people when it's the opposite reaction for the other group?" She didn't wait for an answer. "You see, ignorance causes us to see others within misguided groupings as if there is a permanent concept of good people, bad people, or people we just don't recognize as being either good or bad."

"Yeah, I've learned about that," Troy said, remembering his discussions with Grace. "Seeing people that way totally ignores the fact that things are constantly changing. It's that thing about impermanence, right? Enemies become friends, and friends become enemies, and so viewing people in that limited way is based on ignorance. For example, the guy I think is a really good friend might be the same guy that someone else can't stand because he has the girlfriend the other guy wants. If I see him as a friend, and the other guy sees him as a jerk, then neither of those things has anything to do with the guy himself, but only with the way we see him. How can he be both or neither except based on our different views?"

"It sounds like what you are describing is a self-centeredness," Mrs. Sternau said. "In other words each person in your example holds the belief that there is an independent or inherently existent 'self.' The attachment to this belief is one we all come into human existence clinging to with a very strong habitual force and is considered by some to be our greatest downfall. This attachment also inhibits our compassion, and I think your example illustrates this very nicely. I say this because in the scenario you described, you might determine the jealous young man to be unworthy of your compassion. And why would that be a mistake?"

"Well, the jealous guy is suffering, and, like anyone else who is suffering, he actually needs healing. Just like you'd use medicine for pain or sickness, he needs the medicine of love and compassion," Troy said. "If he's treated with love and compassion, it might make him happier. And then it might help him stop acting like a jerk. Otherwise, he just sets himself up for more suffering."

"That's right," she said. "Jealousy is a form of anger, and, goodness gracious, any form of anger is something to avoid. You see, anger and hatred are extremely powerful emotions that, uncontrolled, will consume our entire mind the way a single flame grows to destroy an entire forest.

"Now, there were moments when Albert and I felt a sense of hopelessness and our determination to not succumb to hatred weakened. During those moments we felt justified in our anger. Of course, there is no use in suppressing anger and pretending you don't feel it. Doing so is no more effective than bailing a sinking ship with only a tiny bucket. Instead, Ruth taught us to remain mindful of *why* anger is so destructive and why it has absolutely no capacity to make anything better. Perhaps more importantly, she taught us to fully understand its causes. She helped us see that no matter what, anger is neither a reasonable or helpful response to anything. You see, anger's energy eclipses the rational part of the brain—the part that has the ability to judge between right and wrong and evaluate consequences. The rational brain becomes thoroughly incapacitated by anger, and the result is something quite insane. Just think about the expression 'blind rage' and you'll understand that anger really is a very forceful energy with no idea where it is going or what it is doing.

"There are obvious reasons why anger is destructive, such as separating us from people we love. Oh my, so often we hear of family members who no longer speak with each other because of some perceived slight or rift. And if you ever tried to get a good night's sleep while angry, then you know it is just about impossible. There simply is no peace in the mind to allow sleep when anger is present. And if vanity is a concern, then one certainly does not want anger to destroy their good looks. Nobody looks good when angry," she said with a smile.

"The Buddha said that no one can make us angry if the seed of anger is not present in our hearts. In truth, we all carry seeds of anger. To spark the seeds into action, all that is necessary is for any of the causes I mentioned before to meet with just the right combination of ingredients." Laughing, she said, "It's like a recipe for a violent brew—all one needs is an average portion of self-centeredness, a cup of attachment, a pinch of jealousy, a pinch of pride, and two scoops of ignorance, and there you have it."

Finishing the last of the lemonade in his glass, Troy said, "I'm sure we've all got a pretty good supply of those ingredients lying around."

"Yes, I think you are quite right. But let us now talk about the more subtle reasons why anger is destructive. You see, unless we fully understand all its facets and mechanisms, it is difficult to turn the tables on anger and be the master of it rather than it being the master of us.

"Since you have been learning about karma you understand the cause and effect nature of how karma works. Virtuous actions generate positive karmic results, and non-virtuous actions generate negative karmic results. Anger's nature is negative. Even if it is only active in the mind with no angry words spoken and no angry actions taken, it will only bring a negative result. If something brings up anger, it is absolutely best not to respond until one reorients their mind to compassion. This will ensure that any actions taken will be based on wisdom.

"Anger is like a bad vapor that permeates space, and the space it permeates is that of the mind. Imagine yourself captive in a room filled with a putrid stench. Then imagine that while in this room you are presented with delicious food. You would not be able to enjoy any pleasant taste because you would be overwhelmed by the awful smell. When anger permeates the mind, its negative aspects become dominant, blocking us from experiencing the sweet things in life. When this happens, all experiences will be fraught with unpleasantness and obstacles. If one is on a spiritual path such as Albert and I strived to be, then one simply cannot progress when anger is active in the mind. And since one's judgment and ability to make wise decisions is impaired by anger, people do things they later regret when under its influence.

"We cannot ignore the negative effect anger has on the body. Medicine cabinets are filled with pills used to treat many of anger's results. As someone who enjoys word games, I have always been amused by only one letter's difference between 'medication' and 'meditation.' Knowing that meditation helps so many afflictions, I wish it could be distributed as widely and readily as medication."

"I've been meditating," Troy announced. "I just began a few months ago."

"Yes, it has helped you, hasn't it?" she asked.

"Yes, it has," he said even though it seemed she already knew the answer.

"Whether we realize it or not, unmonitored thoughts that constantly run through our minds have already become our very wild and unconscious meditation. Through their conscious and unconscious repetition those thoughts are strengthened. When we strengthen thoughts, we strengthen their manifestation in our outer experiences. So it is indeed worthwhile to become conscious, or mindful, of the thoughts we habitually think. Meditation is a way to develop that mindfulness. You see, the mind holds the greatest influence on how we experience life. Our body's influence is secondary to that of our mind unless we are seriously ill or living in conditions where our basic needs for survival are not met. With meditation practice and vigilance to the activity of the mind, we can train our mind to reduce, and even eliminate, the negative force of anger and hatred. You see, when we review the causes of anger as we just did, then we know the list of things we need to stay alert to. Our saving grace will be mindfulness to avoid those causes and wisdom to apply the antidote of love and compassion whenever any cause manifests."

"It must've been really hard to do that when your husband was given that ultimatum with no choice but to leave his job," Troy said.

"Well, we knew we could have chosen to stand on our moral principles and tried to defend ourselves. Albert often revisited that moment of choice in his mind and questioned if he had done the right thing. No matter how many times he questioned his decision, he always arrived at the same answer: that he made the best decision based on all that was known at the time. As time went on, it was clear that everyone was so fearful of being brought up on charges themselves, it would have been extremely difficult to find anyone to defend Albert or a judge to rule in his favor no matter how innocent he was."

"So with all those ingredients for anger you guys had cooking together, how did you and your husband cope?" Troy asked.

"Well, why don't we take a stroll in the garden while I tell you about that? It is too lovely outside to stay in the kitchen." Mrs. Sternau folded her napkin next to her placemat and stood to take her cane.

Troy hadn't planned on spending so much time with Mrs. Sternau. But his afternoon was open, and, even though there was studying to do, he was enjoying the unexpected turn the visit was taking.

"Thank you for lunch, Mrs. Sternau. It was delicious." He cleared the dishes from the table and carried them to the sink.

"Thank you, dear, and please leave the dishes. I'll take care of them later." She used her cane to walk into the next room, took the shawl she had left on the couch near her crossword puzzle, and wrapped it around her shoulders. "Are you ready?" she asked.

"Yes, I am," Troy said.

Troy stopped to look at the photograph on the table by the window of a man smiling, holding a pipe with threads of smoke rising from its bowl.

"Is that your husband?" he asked. He bent lower to see his face more closely.

"Yes," she said. "That's my darling Albert."

"He looks like a nice man," Troy said.

"He was a gem," she said.

Troy opened the porch door and the pair walked slowly across the terrace and down the three stone steps that led to the lower garden. Troy extended his hand for her to take if she needed steadying.

"Are these peonies not just an eyeful of beauty?" Mrs. Sternau stopped to admire the row of large papery white and pink flowers with deep yellow centers that lined the gravel walkway.

"They really are beautiful," Troy said. "I was appreciating your gardens earlier when I was out here working on your gutters."

"Albert and I both loved to garden. But it was Albert who had the artist's eye and the knowledge that serious gardeners need to have." Mrs. Sternau appeared almost as radiant as the pink flowers she was standing near.

"Oh yes, that's right," her voice almost a whisper with the distant tone she had used earlier. "Before I forget," she said, "I must answer your question and tell you how Albert and I found peace after so much we valued had been damaged." She began walking toward the white bench under the beech trees, and Troy walked slowly alongside her.

Mrs. Sternau slowed her pace even more and asked, "If you knew a way to develop an energy of equal force to anger, but one that is controlled and therefore more effective, would you not choose to use it?"

"Yes, of course I would," Troy said as they approached the bench.

Before taking their seat, Troy was ready to brush the dirt and beechnuts from the bench when he noticed it was glistening white and clean. He looked quickly around the garden to see if perhaps this was a different bench from the stained one where he sat earlier, but there was no other bench on the property.

"What happened here?" he asked, not addressing Mrs. Sternau, or anyone else for that matter, and not even expecting an answer.

"What is it, dear? Is something wrong?" Mrs. Sternau asked.

"Um," he wasn't sure how to answer, "I don't know." He quickly wiped his hand on the bench and looked at his palm. His hand was clean. "Um, Mrs. Sternau, this bench was kinda grimy when I sat on it earlier. How'd it get so clean?"

"Oh, nothing to worry about dear," she said. "Just have a seat." She breathed in the garden's air and took in the view of the garden in bloom. "So, where were we?" Reorganizing her thoughts, "Oh yes. Meditation."

> *Whatever wholesome deeds,*
> *Such as venerating the Buddhas and generosity,*
> *That have been amassed over a thousand aeons*
> *Will all be destroyed in one moment of anger.*

> *There is no transgression like hatred,*
> *And no fortitude like patience.*
> *Thus I should strive in various ways*
> *To meditate on patience.*
> *VI. 1, 2*

The time spent with Mrs. Sternau was being shaped by a series of moments that Troy wished to capture into a perfectly stored memory. The day was an unexpected treasure, and he made a mental etching of sorts to hold its essence as best he could.

The two sat quietly on the white bench, steeped in the fragrance, sights, and sounds of the garden that carried its pulse through their senses. Small and less visible activity was diligently at work to provide the perfect balance for the palette of flowers that bloomed year after year. With no conversation to dampen the ambient sounds, the hum of the buzzing bees hovering and dipping into the flowers grew more audible.

"Just look at those magnificent creatures," Mrs. Sternau interrupted the silence. "Watch how they move from flower to flower." She held her palms together as she often did when she felt strongly about something she was saying or when she was moved. "So much depends on these tiny creatures. Just imagine, without them there would be no flowers, and without flowers there would be no seeds, without seeds there would be no nuts, no fruits or berries. And without any of those things there would be no food for animals or for people to survive." She grew quiet again, observing the bees as they went about their activity. "I've seen people frightened by just the sight of a bee. They frantically shoo it away, and then are surprised and upset when it stings. And there are many people who use garden sprays, unknowingly killing the bees with chemicals designed to keep other bugs and weeds away." She watched a butterfly that flew in looping patterns among the bees. "You know, we humans are quite like the bees and flowers in the way we depend on one another. Everyone simply wants happiness, but, sadly, they don't realize that their happiness depends on the happiness of others. Just as it is in dependence upon the bees and flowers that we have food for our planet, it is in dependence upon the happiness of others that we too will have peace and happiness. If we truly understood the value of even a single bee, then we would never seek to kill it. And if we truly understood the value of all beings, we would urgently seek to remove any harmful affliction such as anger or hatred that mistakenly perceives and treats another being as an enemy. You see, we neglect to recognize that those we perceive as enemy are the very ones, like these bees, who help us most."

These weren't entirely new concepts for Troy, although he hadn't considered them in quite this way before. Sitting with Mrs. Sternau, witnessing the world of insects and flowers not as a world separate from his own, but as one that his world depends upon, had a different slant when it brought things like anger and peace into the mix.

"One could say that it took awhile, but Albert had an epiphany during the time we were staying with the Lanimakers. We had been listening to the things Ruth told us about patience and anger. Of course it was all very helpful and good to think about. In fact, it gave us something on an intellectual basis to work with to elevate our experience, so we reflected on all of it a great deal. But as I said before, Albert hadn't been able to completely shed the anger from his mind. Efforts to find a job had been a chain of frustrating experiences. Positive interviews were followed by rejection letters that were a variation on the theme of: 'Dear Professor Sternau, After careful consideration, we regret to inform you that…' Of course Albert knew that meant they had gotten wind of his name having been on McCarthy's list. To be falsely accused, and still carry the burden of conviction, was a very disheartening battle. Anger and frustration would often rise to the surface of his mind during the dark quiet of the night, waking him from his sleep. Once awakened, there were nights he would toss and turn, twisting his blankets into a tangled cocoon, unable to fall back to sleep. Filled with anxiety, thoughts darted about in his mind like bats in summer's dusk. Some nights he would take a flashlight and go outside for walks, hoping the cool air would refresh his perspective. But eventually, Albert and I needed to do more than just listen to Ruth and think about the things she said. We had to actually engage in something that had the ability to untangle the mess of thoughts and emotions that were dampening our hopes for any kind of happiness like we had known before the McCarthy mayhem.

"To help us with something called mind training, Ruth had us memorize this verse:

> 'When I see beings with a bad nature, overwhelmed by their heavy misdeeds or suffering, may I care for them as if I had discovered a jewel treasure, for they are so hard to find.'[2]

"By using meditation to clearly illuminate the reason why those we perceive to be our enemies are actually the very most precious treasures in our lives, one can practice a very powerful compassion. It's an approach that one initially 'tries on' in meditation by

---

2   *The Essence of Mahayana Lojong Practice: A Commentary to Geshe Langri Tangpa's Mind Training in Eight Verses* by Sermey Khensur Lobsang Tharchin, Verse IV

recognizing that the behaviors of one who has harmed you are indeed symptoms of their suffering. A deeper analysis brings about an understanding that the origin of their suffering is ignorance, or the wrong view of how all things and all beings exist. One then begins to see the bigger picture the cycle of ignorance creates. Actions motivated by this ignorance are the cause of more suffering. If we really understand this in all its fullness, then we can't possibly feel anything but compassion—even for someone who has brought us harm. If one puts these things into practice, the liberating peace that follows is truly quite amazing. This is why one who has harmed you becomes a treasure. Perhaps the story of Albert's epiphany will help to explain.

"It happened on a summer afternoon when Albert was sitting in the Lanimaker's backyard, just as we are doing here now. He watched the bees as they darted from one flower to another. He considered that a flower growing open to the sky, with the help of bees and wind, assists in the cultivation and support of life with unimaginable capacity. But a flower grown in isolation, in a small glass terrarium for example, blooms and dies with nothing but a withered stem and compost left behind. Of course the flower in a terrarium is still beautiful while it lives, and the compost is still useful to provide nutrients, but its benefit is far greater when its life is open to all. Albert thought this was something like the greater capacity a person has to benefit the world with a completely open heart, than one shut away in their own self-made terrarium world.

"By harboring anger toward those who had turned their backs on him at his former job or toward McCarthy and his committee, Albert realized that he had gathered them all into the category of enemy. This approach was only capable of delivering more anger and was destroying his peace. His epiphany came when he recognized that by holding this view he was missing something key to a peaceful and more positive experience. Perceiving them as the enemy was like only seeing the bees' capacity to sting without understanding their benefit.

"It would be a very frantic endeavor if one were to run around a neighborhood attempting to kill all the bees, wouldn't it?" Mrs. Sternau asked rhetorically. "And it is an equally frantic endeavor to think one's anger can eliminate everyone who annoys you or brings you harm."

A breeze came as trails of clouds spread over the sun. Mrs. Sternau drew her shawl more snugly around her shoulders. "Instead of seeing those he deemed to be 'enemy' with a capacity to harm him, Albert saw the more subtle mechanisms of karma that were at work amidst the interdependence of all things.

"To understand karma is to understand the nature of cause and effect." She patted Troy reassuringly on his arm, "Oh, I know you have been learning about karma, but I hope you won't mind that I say a bit more about it now."

"Not at all," Troy said.

"Observing nature, it's easy to see that no matter where we look, we are seeing the result of a previous cause," Mrs. Sternau explained. "Of course, the previous cause may no longer be visible, but we do not doubt that it occurred. It is the same with our lives. For example, I have this scar on my hand that came when I carelessly took something from my oven. Because it happened so many years ago, you can see the scar, but you cannot see me burning my hand as I lifted the casserole from the oven. To think the law of cause and effect only applies to some things and not to others, would be as seriously mistaken as to assume gravity applies only to some objects in this planet's atmosphere but not to all. One of the laws of karma is that every cause has an effect, and, furthermore, every cause delivers its like effect.

"Understanding that there could be an enormous collection of karma, Albert realized that all his experiences, the good and the bad, were undoubtedly the result of actions he had committed in the past. Just as you and I cannot remember ourselves as we existed in the womb, we do not remember ourselves in the moment by moments, or lifetime to lifetimes, prior to our conception. Albert's epiphany included a distinct understanding that the negative experience of being falsely accused and without a job was the ripening of his own negative karma. The silver lining was that he could then feel relief knowing that a negative karmic seed had burned away. There is something very empowering and liberating when one takes responsibility for one's past actions, and then takes a different sort of action for the future. For example, one would not want to create more negative karma by reacting ignorantly with anger or blaming others for what happened.

"Albert literally watched his new perspective reveal itself as it was demonstrated by the dance in the garden right before his eyes. It was always there; it simply required time, learning new ways of seeing how things work, reflecting on them, and meditating on them so he could see it. Sitting on the Lanimaker's lawn, he discovered the recipe for patience, the perfect antidote for that venomous brew of anger we talked about earlier. Only this recipe calls for selflessness, or compassion for others, instead of self-centeredness; an understanding of impermanence to replace attachment, pride and jealousy; and wisdom that understands karma, and the interdependence of one and all, as the replacement for ignorance.

"I will never forget Albert's excitement that day." Mrs. Sternau began to laugh. "He began babbling about bees, and pollen, and compassion, and anger, all in such a scramble I couldn't understand a thing of what he was trying to tell me. After he calmed down a bit, he managed to make it clear.

"'We are like the flowers,' Albert explained. 'And others, including those we perceive to be enemies, are the bees on whose wings we spread the pollen either of love and compassion or anger and hatred. By living our lives open to the sky, with a mind of love and compassion, our capacity to bring peace is immense. But if our minds are holding seeds of anger, it is fields of pain and suffering that we will generate. So with that awareness, it is actually in dependence upon these beings that have harmed me that I can experience peace. And it is when I live my life with the mind that wishes to benefit others, that others might also know peace.'

"So you see," Mrs. Sternau said, "meditation can include a very active but very focused kind of thinking, such as Albert's meditation in the Lanimaker's garden. After sorting through the reasoning about why there is an excellent benefit to be gained by replacing anger with love and compassion, one begins to experience the potential for peace. *This* is patience. And the practice of patience absolutely will not fail to deliver the more powerful, controlled energy and force to eliminate anger. After meditating in this active way, one then holds one's focus on the experience of compassion in whatever way comes most naturally. It is through meditation that we can develop a quiet, peaceful mind. The practice prepares us so that, even when we are not in meditation, we will eventually be able to keep a peaceful mind and have immediate access to that focused energy. And with a peaceful mind and its focused energy, it is simply not possible for anger to arise."

"Did things change for your husband after that?" Troy asked. He felt certain the peace he had sensed in the garden earlier must be the result of Professor Sternau's more peaceful mind.

"The immediate change for Albert was within himself," she said. "He no longer tossed and turned at night, he no longer rehashed the injustices of his experiences over and over again or second-guessed his choice to resign from his position. It can take awhile for our outer world to catch up with our inner world, and that was absolutely the case for Albert. In time, he felt that his more peaceful demeanor changed the way others responded to him. His credentials had always impressed people he interviewed with. But when people he spoke with began to seem more inclined to help him find a new teaching position, he wondered if it had been more than McCarthyism that had sabotaged his success."

"Well, how did he finally get his job at the university here?" Troy asked.

"The Lanimakers used to host a summer picnic every August. It was a fabulous tradition that everyone looked forward to each year until the time came when Harold and Ruth were no longer able to manage the preparations. Then a younger couple took over the tradition, but it lacked a certain magic that everyone agreed must have been a special presence in Harold and Ruth's garden." Mrs. Sternau looked into the distance through the woods. "It is amazing how close those memories can feel, and then oh so shocking when I realize how long ago they were."

Troy looked at her hands, one placed lightly over the other, resting on her lap. He noticed the scar that was a pale, thin line on skin that had thinned to merely cover the blue veins that rose like swollen rivers over a web of tendons and bone. He noticed the gold wedding band and small diamond on a ring that had spun loosely off center, and he tried to imagine the graceful hand that accepted Albert's hand in marriage so many years earlier.

Mrs. Sternau's eyes followed the movement of a bird's shadow that slid across the lawn before she spoke again. "It was at the Lanimaker's picnic in August when Albert got to talking to one of the other guests, Lou Raphterson. Lou happened to be a good friend of Stephen Chaversly who was the head of the history department at that time. An introduction was made, and Stephen offered Albert a job to fill a position that had unexpectedly opened for the fall semester."

"How did the McCarthy thing not come up with that guy?" Troy asked.

"Oh, it came up alright," she said. "But Stephen was not one to surrender to fear. Besides, it was becoming apparent, and more widely accepted, that McCarthy's accusations and methods had been flawed.

It just didn't carry the same punch that it had when it all began."

"Do you think it was just good luck and timing then or good karma that he got the job?"

"As I said earlier, nothing exists without a preceding cause. The way things changed for Albert was no exception, including the way he really got the job and his understanding of the nature of karma. The negative karma that had ripened in the McCarthy debacle had expired like a ripened peach dropped from a tree. By practicing patience, he avoided the pitfalls of creating more negative karma in the wake of that experience. His realization of how things really work, and the calm and compassionate state of mind that followed, removed the main obstacle to resuming his career in the world of teaching that he so dearly loved."

Troy felt something that bordered on awe when he considered the string of causes and ripening karma that landed him next to Mrs. Sternau, sitting on the white bench under the beech trees.

Therefore the Mighty One has said
That the field of sentient beings is (similar to)
a Buddha-field,

For many who have pleased them
Have thereby reached perfection.
VI. 112

Troy thanked Mrs. Sternau for lunch, and emphatically refused to accept the folded bills she pulled from her dress pocket. She insisted he take the money, and he insisted he would not, until they both finally agreed it all had been a wonderful way to spend the day and that they really must do it again sometime very soon. He walked with her up the steps to the terrace and to the porch door.

"Before I leave, I want to make sure you have my phone number," Troy said. "Do you have it already?"

"I don't believe I do," she said. "Come on in and you can leave it with me now."

She handed him a small, white card with slots on its edge to slide into the Rolodex wheel she kept by her phone. "Please write your name and phone number here."

For a moment he debated whether she would most easily recognize his name as Troy or Trevor before writing *Troy* and then the number for his cell phone. "Call me anytime," he said. "And if there is ever anything you need help with, I'll be here in a heartbeat," he added, hoping he would always be able to deliver on that offer.

Mrs. Sternau accompanied Troy to the door, thanked him again for his help, and, with a sleepy sigh, announced it was time for her nap. "Naps are very good for the body and mind," she advised him and encouraged him to make a habit of taking naps too. "Now keep an eye on the bees, especially those that come in human form. And remember Albert's story in your meditation and as you go about your daily life. It will help you."

Troy agreed that taking naps and remembering Albert's epiphany both sounded like good advice, and said he would keep them in mind along with all the other important things she told him.

As he began walking from the house back to his truck, the wind picked up, carrying the sweet scent of lily of the valley from the shade of an oak tree and a butterfly to land inside the open rim of the passenger door window.

Before he drove away, Troy texted Maggie to let her know he was just leaving Mrs. Sternau's and that he would be by later to see how her art project was coming along. She texted back that it was going better than she'd hoped and couldn't wait for him to see it. Ordinarily he would have gone directly over to Maggie's, but this afternoon he didn't want to be with anyone for a while. Not even Maggie or his friends. He wanted some solitude and quiet to reflect on the experience of his extraordinary visit with Mrs. Sternau.

Troy followed the road from Mrs. Sternau's house to the entrance of the woods and parked in the small clearing off the road. He walked the trails he had grown to know well as a child until he arrived at the pond. He climbed the rock that protruded into a ledge over the water. Here, the only sounds were of birds, squirrels, and chipmunks rustling in the leaves and the occasional sound of a passing car in the distance. A turtle slipped silently into the water and disappeared into the shimmering brown and green water where flies skimmed tiny rings onto its surface. Troy took a seat on the sunniest patch of rock, and began sorting through and reviewing the things he and Mrs. Sternau had talked about. At least that was his intent. What ensued was a mind that fired off questions that mostly raised more questions.

If everything is a result of a preceding cause, then should I think meeting Grace, Abe, and Mrs. Sternau is like one collective result? Or maybe each meeting is the result of the one that came before—like a result of

the new awareness each one awakened in my mind?
Like, maybe I'm on some kind of causal roll of meet-
ing teachers. When Mrs. Sternau talked about the scar
on her hand, she said we can see her scar but we can't
watch her burn her hand when she took the pan from
the oven. So who knows what's causing all this to hap-
pen? 'Cuz I can't see it. And, oh yeah. Who the hell was
she talking to when her voice would get all soft and dis-
tant? And who cleaned that bench? I couldn't see any
of that either. But does it really matter? Because ev-
erything she told me about the teachings and practices
her husband learned to effectively deal with his anger,
and the things she said about their experiences, felt very
powerful and real. And her husband's epiphany made
a lot of sense—unless someone asked me to explain it,
in which case I probably couldn't get it straight.

But I get it. That's the important part. I get how
I have a choice in every thought, in every action, and
in how I respond to every encounter. I get that based
on whatever action I take in mind, body, or speech,
I will get some version of its like result. I get that if I
feel anger, it's because I'm seeing things all wrong. I
get that if I want peace for myself, I need to generate
peace for others and get rid of the causes of anger in
my own mind. If I want happiness for myself, I have

to want and work for happiness for others. Was that it? Was that everything? And so now what do I do? I think I've got to turn all this into a meditation. I should definitely go see Mrs. Sternau again and really learn it right. Because if I practice all that in meditation, it'll change the way I perceive everything, and everyone too. And, oh yeah, by the way, I don't inherently exist. Yeah, right. Do I really know what the hell that means? Every time I think I begin to get the idea of that, it slips away again.

But that's the deal. That's why I have to meditate on these things. So I can get a handle on how things really exist. I didn't just pop into existence without causes and conditions, and other people didn't just pop into existence, or into my life for that matter, without causes and conditions either. People don't just like me or not like me based entirely on me, because if that were the case, then everyone, without exception, should either really like me or really hate me. And then concepts of friend or enemy or neutral person don't inherently exist either. It's all like some machinery of never ending spokes and gears on wheels that keep turning, and meshing, and turning, and meshing, and moving, and changing. Okay, for God's sake, just get quiet and focus on that thing of being like one of those *flowers. And not like the one flower in the terrarium, but a flower that offers itself to the sky and lets the bees climb on me taking whatever it is they need, because that's what will keep those wheels moving, and meshing in the direction of peace, and—so—is that it? It sounds too simple. But is it?*

His thoughts went round and round like that for quite awhile, until the gnats and mosquitoes began to surround him with all their humming and biting and presented the opportunity to practice not seeing them as annoying creatures. But he wasn't quite getting himself to the loving-them-like-they're-his-precious-mother part of the practice that Grace had told him about. So he took his cue to leave, to find Maggie, and to see the art project she'd been working on all day.

⌒

Whatever (merit comes from) venerating one with a loving mind
Is due to the eminence of sentient beings.
And in the same way, the merit of having faith in Buddha
Is due to the eminence of Buddha.
VI. 115

"Mags?" Troy knocked and waited for Maggie to come unlock the screen door. Since a determined intruder would easily rip the door open, he wondered why she bothered locking it. Except maybe for Natalie, he never felt a stronger desire to protect someone than he did Maggie. He hoped that one day, the turning around he was doing in his own life would lead him to be in the position to provide a home where he and Maggie might build a life together and where she would always feel safe. This hope was the inspiration that encouraged him whenever he questioned whether or not his efforts at school were at all worthwhile.

"It's about time." He heard Maggie's voice before her bare feet and cut-offs came into view on the staircase. "What took you so long?" she asked, opening the door to let him in.

"Sorry, Mags." He wrapped her into his arms. There was no short answer to that question so he changed course. "Did you get a lot done?"

"Yeah, come look," she turned to climb the stairs. "I'm really excited for you to see it."

At the top of the stairs she told Troy to close his eyes while she took his hand and led him into her room where she was painting. "Don't open your eyes yet."

He could hear her moving things around. "Okay," she said. "You can look now."

Immediately, he recognized Abe in the painting. Maggie had painted him standing outside his shop, looking much the way Troy had seen him several times since the first day they met. Abe was leaning against the door to the shop with only a portion of its sign, "Olde and Older," visible within the canvas. With just the right indication of crows' feet and smile lines, and the particular way Abe held his head, Troy could practically hear him laughing. Maggie had a gift for bringing light into her paintings, and the brightness of the day was evident even in the burgundy and gold fibers of Abe's plaid jacket. The enlarged photograph she had used to paint from was tacked onto the wall next to the easel.

"I love it, Mags." Troy stood in front of the painting taking in its details. "You've really captured his Abe-ness. I love the way you got that sparkle in his eye; you know, that almost mischievous glint that makes you wonder what things he knows but just isn't talking about."

"You have no idea how much hearing that comment matters." Maggie stood next to Troy, resting her hand on his shoulder while she tried to see the painting objectively. "I hope my teacher will like it as much as you do."

"I know I don't have a trained artist's eye and can't comment on things like composition or balance and stuff like negative space," he said. "But, in my opinion, I can't imagine your teacher won't love it too."

"Well, I'm bummed that I didn't get to go with you to Mrs. Sternau's, but I definitely needed time to work on this today. If I don't finish this project before next week, I'm in trouble." Maggie stood quietly, slowly twirling a strand of her hair while she looked more closely at her work. "There are just a few more little touches I'll want to add. I've still got time to do that.

"But I'm getting a little antsy," she said. "Let's walk into town. Maybe even see a movie or something? I could go for some popcorn. What do you think?"

"Um, sure," he said. Maggie was pleased with her painting, and he was relieved she wasn't asking him a lot of questions about Mrs. Sternau. He would tell her about the way the day unfolded sometime soon, but for now a movie would be a nice distraction.

"Okay. I want to change out of these clothes," Maggie said. "I'll be ready in a minute."

Troy stretched out on Maggie's bed and rested while he waited for her. She wasn't one to fuss over clothes and makeup, so if she said she'd be ready in a minute, there wasn't much exaggeration involved. He could have easily drifted off to sleep in the lazy light that the gauze curtains breathed into the room with each puff of the evening's humid breeze. The light played with his senses so that images of Mrs. Sternau's garden filled his mind with vivid color, and then something that seemed like an audible impression of her voice startled him back from a dream that had almost begun.

"Hey, Troy," Maggie whispered. "Are you awake?"

"Yup, I am." He sat up. "Are you ready to go?"

"Yeah, are you? You look tired."

"No, not at all," he said. "Just resting my eyes."

"Are you sure?"

"Yeah." He stood up and arched his back, stretching his arms toward the ceiling. "Let's go."

⌒

It is the fault of the childish that they are hurt,
For although they do not wish to suffer,
They are greatly attached to its causes.
So why should they be angry with others?
VI. 45

Meditation was a relatively new practice for Troy, but it was becoming a consistent routine. He carved out time to sit for about twenty minutes each morning to simply follow his breath, quiet his mind, and strengthen his ability to focus. When he first began to practice, he couldn't sit for more than five minutes without feeling restless and squirmy. But little by little, his legs and back became accustomed to holding his posture, and his mind became accustomed to holding its focus. Some days felt more successful than others, but Grace had told him that was to be expected.

We don't notice the day-by-day changes that occur as seasons pass from one to the next. Similarly, Troy's awareness of the changes meditation brought came quietly, in unannounced ways. For instance, there was the day he was stuck in gridlocked traffic when he realized he wasn't one of the drivers slamming on his horn or having temper tantrums in his car. This marked a significant change for Troy, especially when he noticed that instead of being aggravated by the angry drivers, he actually felt sorry for how miserable they were.

In the week following his visit with Mrs. Sternau, Troy was determined to bring the things she taught him into his meditation practice. He had come away from that visit knowing there was more he wanted to accomplish through meditation. There are some meditations known as *calm abiding* for quieting the mind and others known as *analytical meditation* that, based on thorough examination, serve the purpose of making one's understanding and convictions very firm. The recognition of truth arrives by testing things through investigation and by developing wisdom based on intelligent exploration of study, observation, and reflection. So it was into this type of meditation that Troy took things Mrs. Sternau had said and ran them through his own background of understanding.

Mrs. Sternau provided plenty of things to examine and explore, and Troy began by thinking more deeply about karma and impermanence. If we understand impermanence, then we understand the futility of attachment. Relationships aren't static—they change, circumstances change, and people move on in one way or another. There is absolutely no *thing* of this world that will provide lasting satisfaction. Temporary satisfaction, yes, but permanent, no. Enjoy things and be happy in that enjoyment. But the moment one expects lasting happiness from something, which by its own changing nature is incapable of providing lasting happiness, then the set up for pain and future suffering has most definitely been put in place.

With this understanding, we then examine the nature of how things really exist in dependence upon causes and conditions. Every aspect of our lives is ripening karma and the result of causes that we ourselves have generated. Troy was able to see that the origin of negative karma stems from ignorance, the origin of virtuous karma stems from wisdom, and that all actions are rooted in either one or the other. *So*, he thought, *if I am having a bad experience, its origin is ignorance, and if I am having a good experience then its origin is wisdom.*

He reflected more on what Mrs. Sternau said about both happiness and unhappiness arising from the mind. With anger clearly falling within the category of unhappiness, he began to connect the dots to see that by being mindful of thoughts, intentions, and motivations, it must be possible to eliminate the causes of anger. If it's possible to eliminate the causes of anger, then it must be possible to eliminate the causes of all other negative experiences too. And something else she said struck a strong chord of truth for Troy. That the thoughts that run wild and unconsciously through our minds have actually become our personal meditation strengthened through habit. So it is only logical that a habit of mindfulness can help stop the negative causes of anger and hatred, which in turn will strengthen a peaceful mind.

Furthermore, Mrs. Sternau reinforced something both Abe and Grace had explained when they talked about equanimity. Because things like friend or enemy do not inherently exist, it is a wrong view that has one set of rules for friends and another set of rules for enemies. There really is no enemy except for ignorance. Ignorance gets the ball rolling for all other negative experiences to be set in motion. But with equanimity, actions will be based on the wisdom of loving kindness and compassion.

Examining the actual result of anger reveals that there is no positive result from anger. Some might think it is anger that raises awareness to injustice. In truth, it is the result of compassion that one is motivated to alleviate the suffering of those experiencing injustice. The problems come when anger arises and actions taken are fueled by anger, the result of ignorance, rather than by compassion, which is the result of wisdom. With wisdom, it is always possible to apply the beneficial antidote of patience, love, and compassion whenever an angry thought arises. Wisdom gets the ball rolling for all the positive experiences of peace and happiness.

Troy hadn't thought twice to answer Mrs. Sternau when she asked him, if knowing it were possible, would he choose to use an energy of equal force to anger that is controlled and more effective. Of course he would. There was a lifetime of resentments he held at bay, but there were times he simply did not have the reserves to keep them suppressed. Resentments exist only in the mind and nowhere else. Therefore, any attempt to eliminate resentment must also take place within the mind. Professor Sternau's epiphany shed light on a method to eliminate the causes of resentment and anger by demonstrating that everything truly exists in dependence on a preceding cause.

We are like the flowers. And others, including those we perceive to be enemies, are the bees on whose wings we spread the pollen of love and compassion, or anger and hatred. It is in dependence upon beings that have harmed me that I can experience peace. And with a mind that wishes to benefit others, then others might also know peace.

Troy thought of a passage Mrs. Sternau quoted when they were sitting on the white bench in her garden. It was about caring for people who are really nasty and difficult to get along with in the same way you would care for a rare jewel or a treasure that's really hard to find. He didn't think he could consider Maureen to be a rare jewel or treasure, but when he pictured her in his mind and then pictured something in her heart glowing like a beautiful gem, he did notice that his unpleasant feelings began to fall away.

By thinking these things through, Troy became excited about all there was to learn. He recognized how fortunate he had been to meet Grace, Abe, and Mrs. Sternau, and he wanted to deepen the learning he had begun. He decided to ask Mrs. Sternau to recommend books he should read. With the end of the semester approaching, the summer break would be a good time to begin a new kind of study.

⌒

A beggar is not an obstacle to generosity
When I am giving something away,
And I cannot say that those who give ordination
Are an obstacle to becoming ordained.

There are indeed many beggars in this world,
But scarce are those who inflict harm;

For if I have not injured others,
Few beings will cause me harm.

Therefore, just like treasure appearing in my house
Without any effort on my part to obtain it,
I should be happy to have enemies
For they assist me in my conduct of Awakening.

Because I am able to practice (patience) with them,
They are worthy of being given
The very first fruits of my patience,
For in this way, they are the cause of it.
VI. 105, 106, 107, 108

The following week, Maggie and Troy breathed a little lighter. Finals were behind them, and the semester was over with all deadlines met. They felt they had done pretty well on their exams, but they would have to wait another week for grades to come in. They celebrated the semester's end by spending most of Wednesday at the beach.

There was something about the sea air that invited the quiet things waiting to be said. Or maybe it was just the feeling of dissolving into the sand with no other place to go and no reason to wait any longer. With the experience of his unusual visit with Mrs. Sternau a little more settled in his mind, Troy told Maggie about the afternoon they had spent together. He told her the impact of that visit had already begun to change his way of experiencing things. For instance, if he felt irritated, he reminded himself that everything, including the irritating things that show up in his life, is a result of causes he himself participated in creating. If he was feeling upset or discontented, by wishing that his discontent could take suffering away from others, he found he could bring joy into his mind. When feeling joy, he wished for his happiness to spread to benefit all others like the pollen in Professor Sternau's epiphany. This mental rechanneling of his experiences helped to nail down the validity of something Mrs. Sternau had said: that all happiness and unhappiness arise from the mind. He told Maggie that the flipping of the switch that turns everything he experiences into an opportunity to practice compassion was totally in his control. He told her that even as this was all fairly new to him, the things that were typically a source of anxiety or irritation were becoming more subdued in his mind. The most obvious change he noticed was that when he was around Maureen, his mind remained more peaceful, and the overall mood at home was less tense. He struggled to describe the way Mrs. Sternau whispered to someone he couldn't see, until Maggie looked at him dubiously, and then he censored the other details. But when he told her that his ambitions were to study more of the Buddhist teachings, or *dharma,* during the summer, she said that was something she would like to do along with him. Before meeting Troy, her exposure to Buddhist teachings had come only lightly through knowing Abe. From all that she observed, the *dharma* felt very natural, and there was a common sense-ness to it that appealed to her.

"How can you go wrong if all you want is for everyone to experience peace and happiness?" she asked.

"I don't think you can go wrong," Troy said. "I know people worry that other people will walk all over them. But I've read that the Dalai Lama says in a situation where something like that's happening, you've absolutely got to remain strong to stop a wrong action, but at the same time, have only compassion for the person who is doing the wrong action." Troy squinted into the sun to look at Maggie. "He also says to never develop a negative feeling—like anger or wishing harm—but instead to always keep a compassionate attitude toward the person. In other words, you may have to stop the negative action but never lose respect for that person."

"That sounds like it would be really hard to do," Maggie said.

"Of course it would be hard to do." Troy laughed. "That's where practice comes in. So if you practice first in small ways on the little things, then I suppose it's possible that some day when a bigger thing hits, you stand a better chance of handling it well."

"Yeah, I guess." Maggie looked at the backs of Troy's legs. "You're getting burned. Do you want to move into the shade?"

"Nah," he said. "I'll just flip over."

"Here, use some sun screen." Maggie pulled a bottle of lotion from her bag and handed it to him.

"Thanks, Mags." He began spreading the sunscreen on his legs. "You know what else Mrs. Sternau said?"

"Oh my, there's more?" Maggie flipped over to lie on her back too. "Okay, what else did she say?"

"She said naps are really good for the mind and the body." He twisted the cap back onto the bottle and returned it to Maggie. "So I think I'm gonna just close my eyes and snooze. How about you?"

"Um, maybe in a bit," she said. "I brought a book with me, so I'll read while you snooze."

"Okay," Troy said.

⌒

Thus, since patient acceptance is produced
In dependence upon (one with) a very hateful mind,
That person should be worthy of veneration just like
the sacred Dharma,
Because they are a cause of patience.
VI. 111

"What is this crap?" A man's voice broke loudly over the other conversations in the diner. "I didn't order this goddamn sausage. I ordered bacon for Christ's sake."

Troy turned to see who was talking. He felt his adrenaline surge when he saw Maggie biting her lip in that beautiful way she does when she is fighting tears. She stood by the man's table carrying a tray filled with breakfast orders. Unable to speak, she began to lift the plate to return it to the kitchen.

"Now what the hell are you doing?" He began sputtering his rage while the rest of the customers grew quiet. "God dammit, I don't have time to dick around with this shit. Just leave it. But I'll be goddamned if I'm paying for this crap."

Troy was barely aware of having set the bus pan and rag on the table he was clearing before he found himself standing between Maggie and the irate customer.

Troy's thoughts moved faster than ever. *Here it is. Remember what I've been learning. Patience. Stop the negative action but never lose respect for the person. See his suffering and the ignorance that has caused it. Then there's no way I can feel anything other than compassion. The moment I perceive him as enemy, I'll lose all wisdom.*

"Well, what the hell do *you* want, tough guy?" the man said.

But I could kick this guy's ass so fast he wouldn't know what hit him.

No, he admonished himself. *Not an option. Remember cause and effect—seeds of anger grow into fields of pain and suffering. Stop the causes. Just stop anger before it stands a chance to ignite. I've done enough of that. Turn it around. Change the hab-it. What's that recipe? Selflessness. Impermanence. Wisdom. Patience.*

"I'm sorry, the mix up on your order was my mistake," Troy said. "I'll get you a side of bacon, and there will be no charge."

"Fine," the man grumbled. "Bring me a goddamn side of bacon." Noticing most everyone in the restaurant was watching, he looked down at his plate and began to eat.

I can't believe I'm actually feeling sorry for this guy. He looks totally humiliated and uncomfortable. I feel like patting him on the back and telling him everything's okay and not to worry. Probably not a good idea. Don't touch him. It would piss him off all over again.

Troy went into the kitchen, and Theo handed him an order of bacon. "Here you go, my man." He looked deeply into Troy's eyes and said, "I don't know how you did it or what you did, but whatever it was I'm glad you did it." He laughed nervously, "I was getting ready to go break up a fight."

"Let's just hope he's happy with the bacon," Troy said as he took the plate. Leaving the kitchen, he caught

Maggie's eye from across the room. When she smiled at him, he hoped that meant she was okay.

Troy set the plate of bacon on the table. "Here's your bacon. Let me know if I can get you anything else." He filled his water glass thinking, *it is only in dependence upon this man and others that I can experience peace. And with the wish to benefit others, then they might also know peace.*

Holding that thought in his mind like a mantra, Troy went back to the table he had been clearing and to catch up on the others that emptied during all the commotion. Several tables needed to be set for new customers waiting by the door.

He didn't know how long she had been sitting there before he noticed Mrs. Sternau at her table with an order of fruit cup, cottage cheese, and a cup of coffee.

"Good morning, Mrs. Sternau," He couldn't have been happier to see her. "I lost track of the week. It must be Thursday. How are you?"

"Oh, I am doing very well, dear, thank you," she answered. "I know you are busy now, but perhaps you and Molly might like to come for tea this weekend. I came across one of Albert's books that I think you would like to have. I know he would approve of my giving it to you."

"Really? I'd be honored, thank you," he said. "I'll tell Maggie. I know she'll want to come too."

"Well, can you come on Sunday afternoon?" she asked. Troy noticed that she pressed her hands together the way she had when they had been in the garden talking together.

"We're finished here by three o'clock, is that okay?"

"Let's plan on four o'clock then," she said. "That's a perfect time for tea."

"That sounds great," he said while keeping an eye on the other tables.

Troy had told Maggie that he would take over the job of serving the angry customer, so when he saw his coffee cup was getting low he excused himself from Mrs. Sternau to offer him more.

"No thanks," the man said without looking up. "But tell the young lady I'm sorry."

Another customer asked Troy for more coffee, and by the time he returned the pot to its place on the counter, both the man and Mrs. Sternau had left. Troy opened the door to catch up with Mrs. Sternau to say goodbye, but her car was gone.

My Darling,

Yesterday evening from our seat in the porch I searched the garden for fireflies but alas it is too early for their debut.

How pleased you would be this morning to see our garden teeming with honeybees working steadfastly so that not one flower is neglected.

The neighbor's cat came stalking something that caught its eye. The poor thing lost its prey so proceeded to rest in the grass where the clover and buttercups grow. Here, I thought, is peace. Great peace.

Loving you always,
Esther

For myself and for my friends
I want no suffering, no disrespect,
No harsh words and nothing unpleasant;
But for my enemies, it is the opposite.

The causes of happiness sometimes occur
But the causes for suffering are frequent.
Without suffering, there is no renunciation.
Therefore, mind, you should stand firm.
VI. 11, 12

"Troy, I want to say so much but feel completely speechless," Maggie said. Their shift was winding down, and everyone was finishing their last few tasks before they could leave for the day. "But, I want to thank you for taking over with that obnoxious creep."

"No problem, Mags," Troy said, following Maggie from table to table. As she cleaned the tables, he flipped the chairs upside down onto the tables so the floor could be washed. "He told me to tell you he was sorry."

"Really?" Maggie stopped wiping the table she was working on. "I'm surprised he's capable of an apology." She got back to cleaning the tables. "I hope he never comes here again."

"Don't worry about it, Mags. If he does, I'll take care of him. You know I've always got your back," Troy said, trying to lighten things up.

"You handled him really well, Troy," Maggie said. "I was so caught off guard and stunned, I almost started crying." Her voice broke as she spoke. "I hate when that happens. It's like I have no control, and the tears just start like they've got a mind of their own. And the last thing I want to do is burst into tears 'cuz then I can't even defend myself." She took a deep breath, and the sigh that was almost a moan was the sound of her emotions kicking in. "We've had other rude customers, but that guy was the nastiest, raunchiest asshole I've ever come across." She moved faster as she worked, and when she finished wiping the tables she began putting the last few chairs on the tables. The faster she moved, the louder each chair slammed against the tabletops. "He's damn lucky I didn't dump the tray of food onto his big, fat, ugly, old head," she announced with a loud final crash of the last chair.

Troy hadn't seen Maggie upset like this before and was unsure how to respond. He knew from his own experience that the less others said when he was angry, the less likely it would escalate into something more. So he didn't say anything.

"I hope he eats so much goddamn greasy bacon and eggs that he dies of a goddamn freaking heart attack." She looked at Troy, her eyes filled to their brim with tears. "I know what I'm saying is really mean, Troy, but don't even think about getting all Buddhisty on me. Just save it," she yelled, and then covering her face with her hands, she sobbed.

Troy felt her sadness like it had punched a hole in his heart. She had seemed okay earlier when he saw her smile from across the room. And so much for her claim to be speechless.

Just because she didn't want to hear any Buddhist inspired thoughts didn't mean they didn't enter his mind. Of course the last thing she'd want to hear was that karma ripens without discrimination, and apparently one of her own karmic seeds had met its perfect conditions. That also meant she wouldn't want to hear any advice about taking some sort of pleasure or relief in the fact that having ripened, the karma is over and done with. Like waking from a bad dream, its power is lost. He was having a harder time not cautioning her that any anger she nurtures toward the man creates new negative karma. To go down that path would only add to her anger, which would only increase the harm. So he kept quiet, wishing he could take away all the sadness, hurt, anger, and anything else that brought her pain. He couldn't bear to see her hurt, but there was nothing more to do than to simply hold her. And as he felt the fabric of his shirt against his skin growing damp from her tears, that is all he did for as long as it took for Maggie to soften and for her tears to stop.

Maggie pulled a fistful of napkins from the chrome dispenser on the counter. "I'm sorry, Troy." Blowing her nose, her voice smothered into the napkins. "I just don't know how to deal with people like that. It's like I have no survival skills or something, and it frustrates the hell out of me that I don't know how to defend myself when someone's in my face like that."

Troy found it ironic that in the face of hostility, Maggie's challenge was the complete opposite of his own. Had the identical scenario unfolded only a year earlier, he would've grabbed the man from his chair and pummeled him to the floor within seconds. Had he been drinking, it would've been much worse. Just thinking about the impulse to fight brought a rush of adrenaline. Was there anything fundamentally different between the root of Maggie's feeling she was incapable of defending herself and the root of his impulse to become violent in the presence of anger? The man wasn't threatening their lives, but he threatened something Mrs. Sternau, Abe, and Grace might all describe as a wrong perception of self and other. Troy needed to learn more about this wrong perception. His initial understanding was only fleeting, and, although he tried, he couldn't quite get a fix on it in his mind. He was eager to have Maggie join him in studying, but, since she told him not to get all "Buddhisty," he questioned if she really wanted to learn. He felt another stab at his heart when she banned him from referencing the very teachings he had drawn on to calm things down. But maybe that stab in his heart was just an indication that his wrong perception of a self, the one that sets people up for feeling hurt or defensive, was activated. Grace taught him a practice to counteract this. Remembering that it had helped him before, he decided to use it again.

He brought his attention to Maggie and then to his breath. As he breathed, he imagined he could draw away all her sadness by breathing it into himself, like a dark vapor, letting it extinguish the self-centered view that was the source of his own suffering. Then he visualized the more powerful and brilliant flame of love and compassion filling his heart, and imagined it, in the form of white light, leaving his heart to fill hers. In his mind's eye, he saw her as if she were infused by light, relieved of all her sadness and filled with peace. As he moved through this practice, it was only peace that then filled his heart as well. It felt as if time had either stood still, or simply vanished, until something that needed no words moved them back into the realm of ticking clocks and the awareness that it was time to go.

They said their goodbyes to Theo and walked quietly together out the back door of the diner. As they pulled away from their parking spot in the shade, they saw Theo leave the diner carrying pieces of bread that he began to scatter for the birds. A row of small brown birds perched along the roof's ledge were calculating their best shot for some morsel of food while others swooped in for landings practically at Theo's feet. Troy thought Theo couldn't have looked any happier if he tried.

Furthermore, suffering has good qualities:
Through being disheartened with it,
arrogance is dispelled,
Compassion arises for those in cyclic existence,
Negativity is shunned and joy is found in virtue.
VI. 21

Maggie's mood brightened when Troy told her that Mrs. Sternau had invited them to tea on Sunday afternoon. An invitation for tea with Mrs. Sternau felt like something special and formal, and Maggie wondered if there were important manners they should know. "You know, things like extending our pinky fingers when we sip from the teacup or not sitting down before she's invited us to sit."

"She's not all that formal, Maggie," Troy began and then changed his mind. "Come to think of it, maybe you're right. When I had lunch with her, she used a fork and knife to eat her sandwich."

"See?" Maggie laughed. "I knew it." Twisting a piece of her hair between her fingers, she thought for a moment and said, "We'll bring her some pretty cut flowers, and maybe I'll bake her some crumpets or something. I think that's what people are supposed to have with afternoon tea."

"Crumpets?" Troy asked.

"Yeah, crumpets," she said, enjoying the feel and sound of the word. "They're kinda like English muffins, only I think they're better. I'll find a recipe online." She stopped twisting her hair and looked at Troy like something terrible had just happened. "What'll I wear? I think I should wear a dress or a skirt, don't you think?"

"Maggie, I don't think she cares what we wear," Troy laughed. "I think she just wants us to come for tea." Soaking in the feeling of sun and wind that poured through the window he added, "You're beautiful no matter what you're wearing, Mags."

"Well, beauty's in the eye of the beholder, so I think I'm damn lucky you're the one beholding me. Especially today." She leaned as close to him as her seatbelt permitted. "And just in case you don't already know, I think you're beautiful too."

Back at Maggie's house they filled two tall glasses with juice and took their drinks onto the back porch. It wasn't much of a porch, and it wasn't much of a view, but it was home for now, and they were happy to have a place to rest and put their feet up. It was a very different scene than the one Troy imagined when he pictured Mrs. Sternau and her husband sitting together on their porch, but he thought the feelings shared between him and Maggie might be close to the same. Holding Maggie's hand, he thought it rested perfectly in his own, like a pearl in its shell. He remembered the image of Mrs. Sternau's hands when he sat with her on the white bench in her garden. He hoped that years from now, after time had left its marks on their own hands, that they would find themselves sitting together just like this on a peaceful summer day on a porch with a garden view.

⌇

For example, when a fire in one house
Has moved into another house,
It is right to get rid of straw and such things
That will cause the fire to spread.

Likewise, when the fire of hatred spreads
To whatever my mind is attached to,
I should immediately get rid of it
For fear of my merit being burned.
VI. 70, 71

On Sunday afternoon a dozen crumpets were nested in a basket, wrapped in a colorful cloth, being kept warm on Maggie's stovetop. Since the recipe said the baking powder in the batter needed more than an hour to "foam," Maggie arranged to have her lunch shift covered so she could leave work early to prepare the batter. The instructions said she would need special rings to form the crumpets' shape and that she could make them by removing the tops and bottoms from shallow cans. When she poured the batter into the greased rings, she was relieved to see holes form as the crumpets cooked on the griddle. The recipe emphasized that these holes were the important part of the crumpets' texture to soak up the butter and marmalade that would be spread on top. Earlier, when Troy asked why she was making so much fuss over everything, she argued that it wasn't to impress Mrs. Sternau. It was because over the couple years she'd been working at the diner, she had grown very fond of her. "Maybe baking for people is just one of the ways I let them know I appreciate them. Like the time I baked brownies for Abe." When she placed the crumpets in the basket and admired their perfectly round shapes dotted with perfect, little craters, she realized the truth was that it made her pretty happy too.

She chose the sleeveless lavender dress with the scoop neck made of fabric that didn't need ironing. It was light, comfortable, and not too short. When she pulled her hair back into a silver barrette, she thought she actually looked the way a guest of Mrs. Sternau's ought to look when invited for tea.

Then she remembered the flowers. She had forgotten to stop at the store on her way back from work. She texted Troy asking if he could pick up a bouquet from the market on his way over to get her. He texted back that he had gone home to shower and change, and he happened to be talking to his father who told him to just cut some daisies and roses that were blooming in their backyard.

Maggie found a length of satin ribbon that she kept in a drawer with spools of thread and scissors and rummaged through a basket in her closet where she found tissue paper with mauve and gold print. When Troy arrived, she wrapped the flowers in the paper and used the ribbon to tie everything into an arrangement that looked at least as lovely as one they might have bought.

⌒

Although I may live happily for a long time
Through obtaining a great deal of material wealth,
I shall go forth empty-handed and destitute
Just like having been robbed by a thief.

Surely material wealth will enable me to live,
And then I shall be able to consume transgressions
and do good—
But if I am angry on account of it
Will not my merit be consumed
and transgressions increase?
VI. 59, 60

Orchestral music played loudly inside Mrs. Sternau's house. When the doorbell remained unanswered, Troy knocked sharply on her screen door.

"That music's kinda dramatic, don't you think?" Maggie whispered. "I feel like we're characters entering a movie or something."

Troy agreed. It wasn't unreasonable to think today's visit might carry the same otherworldly quality that his first visit had.

"Mrs. Sternau?" He called as he knocked again.

"Oh, yes, dear, I'll be right there," her voice came from the other room. The music's volume was lowered before Mrs. Sternau came to the door. Wearing a white cardigan sweater buttoned over her shoulders like a small cape, she seemed to lean only lightly on her cane while she opened the door. "Come in, please. How lovely to see you both," she said. Her voice sounded at once strong and frail if such a thing is possible.

Troy handed her the wrapped bouquet. "Here are some flowers from my father's garden."

"Why, thank you." She brought the flowers closer so she could smell them. "Oh, the roses smell divine. Come with me into the kitchen while I put them in water."

In the vase, the roses and daisies were a perfect complement to the simple elegance that was already arranged on the kitchen table. A china teapot, three matching cups and saucers, sugar bowl, small pitcher filled with cream, and a plate of cookies were all on a tray that Mrs. Sternau asked Troy to carry to the porch.

"Please have a seat," Mrs. Sternau said after the tray had been set on the glass-topped coffee table.

It took a little shifting of things, but Maggie found a spot to place the basket of crumpets and introduced them with the subdued pride of a scientist announcing a new discovery.

"Oh, how marvelous." Mrs. Sternau pressed her hands together. "I haven't had crumpets since Albert and I visited London decades ago." She opened the cloth that wrapped them. "Oh, for heaven's sake, they're still warm. Wonderful!" She reached for her cane to stand. "We must have some marmalade and butter."

"Please don't get up, Mrs. Sternau," Maggie said. "If you tell me where to look, I'll get the marmalade and butter."

"Well, you won't have to look far, dear. I keep a plate of butter on the counter. The marmalade is on the inside shelf of the refrigerator door. There are several jars; choose whichever you like best. Oh, and we'll need some knives as well. You can find knives in the drawer to the left of the sink. Thank you, Molly dear."

The names Mrs. Sternau called them by had become so interchangeable that neither Maggie or Troy registered a difference as to whether they were being addressed as Maggie, Molly, Trevor, or Troy. It really didn't matter. She seemed to draw on "dear" as the perfect substitute for any name when none other came to mind.

There were no pinkies raised as the tea was sipped, but a great deal of care went into the spreading of softened butter and gooey apricot marmalade, and there was a collective silence when Mrs. Sternau took her first taste. There was no poker face hiding the look of hopefulness that lit Maggie's face watching for signs of approval.

"Oh, absolutely heavenly," Mrs. Sternau said. She spoke with the talent of one who had mysteriously mastered the art of not speaking with their mouth full, even when not finished chewing.

Their conversation followed all the contours of polite getting-to-know-more-about-one-another with Mrs. Sternau leading the way. She had a lot of questions for Maggie and was an enthusiastic audience for Maggie's interest in art. She knew just enough about art history and had an aesthetic sensitivity that knew all the right questions to ask.

Savoring the delicious taste of tea and crumpets and the experience of listening instead of talking, Troy learned more about Maggie's dedication to art and how she viewed her every day surroundings as creative inspiration. There were things he hadn't fully appreciated before, like the consideration she gave to light, shadow, and texture, or to things like perspective and space.

"Oh yes, how could I forget?" Mrs. Sternau asked no one in particular. At least no one Troy could identify, although he did recognize the almost whispered tone of voice. He looked anxiously at Maggie to see if she had noticed. He remembered her skepticism the day at the beach when he told her about his first visit with Mrs. Sternau and described how she appeared to be talking to someone or something only she could see.

Because it will hinder my worldly gain—
Even if I do not want this,
I shall have to leave my worldly gains behind
And my wrongdoing alone will remain unmoved.
VI. 55

"Troy, darling," she didn't call him Trevor. Maybe she made a point to study the Rolodex card he had left for her. "I want to commend you for the marvelous way you calmed the customer that was so aggressive to Molly."

She turned her attention briefly to Maggie, "Molly, dear, I am so sorry you were on the receiving end of that exchange. I'm sure it was an absolutely dreadful experience for you."

"Thank you," Maggie said. "You're right, it was pretty dreadful."

And then speaking to Troy again, "Watching you, darling, was like watching Albert in his most glorious moments. It was only after integrating things we learned from Ruth, and the texts we studied, with hours of serious contemplation and meditation that he was able to yield such poise." The blue rings that circled the brown of her eyes shimmered in the low afternoon light. "You were simply sublime, and I rejoice in the way you demonstrated your understanding of so many important things that we talked about the other day. When I saw the way you intervened, I knew immediately that I wanted you to have a book that had been one of Albert's favorites." She lifted a small book the color of faded tangerine from the end table next to where she sat. "There were many books Albert read and valued, but he felt this book embodied the entire Buddhist path with succinct and clear advice especially well. Albert used the short passages from this book in his daily practice by reading, reflecting, and meditating on one each morning. You can see he had several favorites by the corners he turned down on certain pages." She opened the book to one of the dog-eared pages and read out loud, slowly emphasizing each word's importance:

"The indivisibility of clarity and emptiness is like the reflection of the moon in water; there is no attachment or obstruction of any kind..."[3]

She stopped reading and turned the book over, resting Albert's marked page open against her lap. She lowered her head, gazing toward her hands she placed one within the other, and gently moved her wedding ring and diamond back to its more centered position. It was not an awkward silence by any means, but a potent silence that felt to Troy as if it held the very force of life itself. In the way a yawn passes from person to person, both Maggie and Troy lowered their heads as if in reverence to some presence that filtered through the porch screens with the amber honey light that comes just before sundown. And from a tree in the garden, the warbler's song filled the silence as if also made of light, traveling free from the bird that sang it.

When Mrs. Sternau spoke again, even the sound of her voice seemed to leave the silence undisturbed. "We know that life is short and precious, and that upon

---

3   *One Hundred Spiritual Instructions to the Dingri People from Pha Dampa Sangs rgyas, a Buddhist teacher who came from India to Tibet in the last part of the eleventh century.* Edited and translated by Lozang Jlampsal, PhD and David Kittay, PhD Ladak Ratnashridipika 2011

our death we will leave our cherished bodies and those whom we love behind. And of course there will be those who depart before us. It is our lot to either live in grief, denial, and despair, or strive to comprehend our true nature. It is our grave mistake to view anything, or anyone, as existing in any way more fixed or self-sufficiently than the moon's reflection on the water. This does not mean, of course, that nothing exists—only that things don't exist the way they appear. The moon is not found when its reflection is scooped from the water. Nor is the light found on the moon itself, as it makes no light of its own."

She lifted the book from her lap, glanced at the open page again, and thumbed through the other pages before she closed it. "Albert was several years older than I, so I shouldn't have been surprised when he died so many years before me. Our life together had been so vibrant that I just hadn't expected his passing to come as early as it did. Of course I had an awareness of life's fragility, but the mind has a naïve belief that it has accepted things like death and impermanence until it lands on one's own doorstep. I believe if one wants to live meaningfully and joyfully, then one must shake off their squeamishness about the topic and consider one's own death. Ironically—or maybe not—it can serve as a spotlight by illuminating the things that are truly important in life. We miss the boat day after day by preparing for everything except the inevitability of death. We prepare for vacations or positioning ourselves for what we think will be an indestructible career. Or maybe there are things like renovations to a house or another restaurant to try. Oh, by all means, enjoy doing those things; they are part of life, and one obviously must participate in this world. But do them with wisdom. Know that there is no such thing as an indestructible career for instance, and, that while you enjoy the vacation, it is not the vacation itself that is bringing you joy. It is something more, including the quality of mind you bring with you on the vacation. By preparing for death, I'm not talking about things like life insurance policies and wills. Indeed, both can be beneficial, so I'm not suggesting they be neglected. What I am talking about is cultivating the wisdom to meet death for what it is, like slipping into another day carrying the accumulations of the day before. We can do this by meditating on the certainty of death, the uncertainty of when it will happen, and the certainty that when it does happen, none of those things, our bodies, or anyone else for that matter, will be able to help us. You see, it is only the most subtle mind that will determine our experience at the time of death and all that follows, because it is only the most subtle mind that stays with us. I use the term 'us' very sloppily because it is very difficult for us in our present state to separate our true nature from an illusion we simply can't seem to help but hold of ourselves. Consider it as continuing energy that you might picture as a tiny little bundle of DNA loaded with all the ingredients you've put into it over countless lifetimes, and that will very precisely manifest its pattern as it moves along. As we deepen our study and understanding through meditation, we will know our infinite connection to all, and therefore will feel only love and want only happiness for all beings. It may take awhile to arrive at this understanding, but, once there, one finds a rather spontaneous experience of love not unlike being filled blissfully with awe when seeing something of extraordinary beauty. We can call this understanding 'wisdom,' and it brings a positive experience whether one is on the brink of death or of birth." She laughed. "And really, darlings, we are always on the brink of both until we eliminate everything that clouds that perfect understanding.

"I should mention the main offender clouding our ability to reach that perfect understanding is what we call self-grasping. I'm sure it is a strange sounding term, but it is used to describe the mistaken mind that believes something called an 'I' or a 'self' exists independently—like a small child might believe the moon's reflection in the water is in fact the moon. And we cling to this belief in such a way that we compulsively do things with a primary motivation to benefit ourselves and those whom we love and approve of. Things like acquiring wealth for ourselves, fighting enemies to protect ourselves, stealing from others so we can have something more, competing with others so we appear great, and so on. These harmful actions and others like them fall into a category called self-cherishing, and they will bring the guaranteed result of suffering and discontent. It isn't until we learn to exchange our association of the self with that of the other and practice things like the generosity of giving and loving kindness for the benefit of others, that we will absolutely experience true happiness. This intention to benefit others develops the mind of wisdom, and it would be nothing more than ignorance to waste the opportunity we have now, in our present lives, to develop this kind of mind. Imagine the different outcome produced by the most subtle mind which carries the negativity of self-grasping, and the most subtle mind which, free from self-grasping, exclusively carries the DNA of wisdom and compassion."

Troy felt the muscles around his throat tighten and a sinking feeling that pulled from somewhere deep in his heart. With all her talk about death, was this a final teaching, and was Albert's book a final bequest? Mrs. Sternau's white hair and fair skin brushed with rouge had that beautiful, shimmering quality unique to elderly people of appearing to be practically translucent in certain light. The sinking in Troy's heart opened like a bottomless drop to nowhere. It was distinctly fear. Holding the teacup within his two hands, the same unimaginable dark void that swallowed him whole when he heard Jason had been killed was breathing its cold air on the back of his neck. He feared he might begin to weep if he saw the kindness in Mrs. Sternau's face, so he locked his eyes on his practically empty cup of tea. Troy hadn't considered that even just the thought of losing Mrs. Sternau could be so heartbreaking. Scared by his emotions, he began mentally shaming himself out of them. Years of self-humiliation made it the reflexive thing to do when he felt like crying. *Toughen up and be a man, for God's sake*, he told himself before unleashing a string of condemning adjectives. There's loss, and there's loss; and he ridiculed himself for being so small minded to think his own experience of loss had been monumental. After all, there are entire populations that suffer daily loss much greater than he had the capacity to even imagine. Churning anger replaced the threat of tears. The anger he aimed solely at himself was emboldened like a vicious dictator. Then he saw it. Staring into the last bit of tea, he saw it all in an instant.

Noticing the tea stains lining the inside of the cup, Troy recalled something Abe said the afternoon they sat together in the coolness of the early spring sun. He could practically hear Abe's voice again explaining why, as a result of karma, we have habitual ways of perceiving—or strong karmic imprints—that set the stage for the Three Poisons of attachment, anger, and ignorance. Collected over lifetimes, these karmic imprints remain in the mind the way tea will stain the inside of a cup until we do something to eliminate them. Troy thought this must be like the most subtle mind Mrs. Sternau was talking about. Abe also told him that if he ever finds himself aggravated or unhappy, he could be sure that at least one of the Three Poisons had infiltrated his mind. Troy realized that within a matter of seconds all Three Poisons were doing their thing. Ignorance laid the foundation for the mistaken perception that Mrs.

Sternau must exist in some permanent way, which gave rise to clinging attachment, which gave rise to sadness, which gave rise to anger. 'Suffering caused by ignorance,' Abe told him, 'includes not recognizing that everything changes and that even suffering itself is impermanent.' That was when Abe was talking about The Four Noble Truths. He told him that the first two Noble Truths say there is suffering and that there are causes of suffering. The last two say that because there are causes, the causes can be stopped, and therefore suffering can end; and the way to stop the causes is taught in what is known as the path.

The coming together of these things struck Troy in such a way that he almost had the impulse to laugh. He thought we must all be on a path to somewhere determined by the course our minds direct. If the mind is clear, the path will be clear. If the mind is angry, the path will be angry. A mind of peace is the path to peace. And whatever quality fills the mind, including those stains from forever ago, will determine its experience. It's not all that complicated. Like everything else, the mind changes moment by moment, and Troy realized the chain of thoughts he'd just run his mind through demonstrated The Four Noble Truths in a

How Patience Works

flash of time. It was clear that the causes for all he experiences are entirely in his control to create. Albert's life was changed by the realization that it was in dependence upon those who harmed him that he would find peace. Troy realized that it is also in dependence upon those who have achieved a level of mastery to teach that we can gain the wisdom to stop the nonsense of doing the same things over and over again, perpetuating the cycle of ignorance.

He heard Mrs. Sternau's voice in its absent-minded way of whispering her thoughts out loud again, "Yes. Yes. That is quite right."

He looked up from his teacup and met Mrs. Sternau's eyes, noticing they were moistened by tears. "Please Troy, take this book." She supported it with open palms as she passed it to Troy. "I hope you will find it helpful in the way my dear Albert did and, as years go on, that it will remind you of our lovely visits together." She patted the seat cushion for punctuation. "And I hope there will be many more visits with both of you. Please, we must do this again."

She looked first at Maggie and then Troy. "Now if you'll pardon me, I am very sleepy and think I need to rest. I'm up with the birds each morning, and, since

I missed my nap today, I'm afraid the day has caught up with me."

Maggie began putting the dishes onto the tray. "We'll take care of cleaning up, Mrs. Sternau," Maggie said, trying to conceal the alarm she felt seeing Mrs. Sternau suddenly so tired. If she could have, she felt she would have taken her in her arms and carried her wherever she wanted to be.

Troy took the tray into the kitchen and began washing the china. Living with Maureen, he'd learned that fine china definitely does not go in the dishwasher.

Maggie slipped her arm around Mrs. Sternau's and walked with her slowly from the porch into the room where books filled the shelves. A blanket was folded neatly at the end of the couch by the coffee table where the day's newspaper, a magnifying glass, and a pencil were spread about.

"Thank you dear. This is where I like to rest," Mrs. Sternau said, releasing her arm from Maggie's. She moved so gracefully Maggie thought she lowered herself onto the couch like a feather floating to a pond with barely a ripple on the water.

Troy left the dishes draining next to the sink, dried his hands, and went back to the porch for the book Mrs. Sternau had given him. It was probably only the smell of mulch and peat in the garden when Troy thought for a moment that he smelled pipe tobacco. Holding the book in his hands, he went outside to check on the gutters and to see the garden as the tiger lilies were beginning to close their blooms. He watched the white bench surrender to shadows darkening under the leaves of the beech tree and imagined a time when Professor Sternau might have stood in the same place doing the same thing.

As he turned to go back inside, Maggie met him in the doorway. "Mrs. Sternau's pretty tired, we better get going," she whispered.

"Okay," Troy said, pulling the door closed behind him, but the latch in the door wasn't latching properly. He stopped to jiggle the knob in order to loosen it and then closed the door.

"Mrs. Sternau, thank you for tea and for this amazing book." Troy pressed the book between his hands. "It's got a really special place in my heart already, and I'm incredibly honored to have it."

"You're most welcome," she said.

He knew she was tired, but something in Troy didn't sit well with leaving her alone. So he settled for the option of coming back the next day and asked if it would be okay to stop by to fix her porch door.

"Yes dear," she said. "That darn door has been troublesome for the past several weeks. I think it might have something to do with the humidity. But if you have time to work with it, I would be most appreciative."

"Yup, I have time," Troy said. He noticed her reaching for her cane. "Don't get up. We'll let ourselves out."

"You two are such dears," Mrs. Sternau said. "Thank you for the gorgeous flowers and the delicious crumpets. My, what a joy your visit has been."

"For us too," Maggie said. "Thank you. Get some rest, and we'll see you soon."

Troy was accustomed to some of Maggie's out-of-left-field ideas, but he wasn't ready for the idea she had after leaving Mrs. Sternau's house.

"Let's go for a run when we get home," she said.

"A run?" Troy asked. "Since when are we runners?"

"Well, I think we should start," Maggie said. "Listening to Mrs. Sternau talk about dying and stuff, I got to thinking we should be taking better care of ourselves."

"She didn't tell us all that so we'd take better care of our bodies," Troy said. "She told us that so we'd take better care of our minds."

"Yeah, well guess what?" Maggie asked not leaving room for an answer. "We're gonna need healthy bodies in order to live long enough to get our minds as on top of things as hers is. And did you happen to notice that even though she uses a cane she's in pretty good shape? She's got to be over eighty and maybe even close to ninety, don't you think? I want to be doing as well as she's doing when I get to be her age... *if* I get to be her age. So we've got to do stuff like eat better and take up some exercise for our hearts and lungs."

"No way, Mags," Troy said. "You've gotta be kidding. I hate running."

"Oh, come on, Troy. The most exercise we get is carrying food around on trays, and that'll just make us all lopsided or something." She hadn't expected him to be so set against running. "I suppose we could go to yoga classes. At least that would balance our bodies out."

"Forget it," he said. "I'll run with you." He didn't want to admit it, but when he was struggling to keep up with Abe carrying furniture out of a house, he knew he should do something to get into better shape. He just never got around to doing anything about it.

"Really?" She was pleased. "Okay. So, drop me at my house and I'll change while you go home and get your running stuff."

"Okay," Troy said, not in the least bit enthusiastic about the plan. When he considered how disappointed she'd be if he dug his heels in and refused, being agreeable was a little easier.

"Let's go to the track over by the schools. They keep it lit in the evenings," Maggie said as they pulled into her driveway.

"Okay," Troy said. "I'll be back to get you in a bit."

"Thanks." She hesitated and before closing the door said, "Pizza's got some healthy ingredients in it. Let's go for pizza and salad afterwards."

"It's sounding better all the time," Troy laughed.

~

Both the weapon and my body
Are the causes of my suffering.
Since the other gave rise to the weapon,
and I to the body,
With whom should I be angry?

How Patience Works

If, in blind attachment, I cling
To this suffering abscess of a human form
Which cannot bear to be touched,
With whom should I be angry when it is hurt?
VI. 43, 44

Troy pulled a pair of gym shorts from his drawer that he had used in high school for soccer practice. Simply feeling the fabric against his skin brought the hint of memory of how good it felt to run tirelessly during games. Lacing up his sneakers, he was a little surprised to find he was actually looking forward to getting a taste of that feeling again. He took his keys from the dresser next to the book Mrs. Sternau had given him. Keys in hand, he stopped long enough to read one of the pages Professor Sternau had marked.

"Attachment and hatred are like the traceless path of a bird; don't get absorbed in experience..."[4]

He read it again, this time softly speaking the words out loud to absorb their meaning. The first thing

---

4   *One Hundred Spiritual Instructions to the Dingri People from Pha Dampa Sangs rgyas, a Buddhist teacher who came from India to Tibet in the last part of the eleventh century.* Edited and translated by Lozang Jlampsal, PhD and David Kittay, PhD Ladak Ratnashridipika 2011. Pg. 48

that came to mind was that although a bird may leave a traceless path in the sky, its shadow can be seen on the ground. But shadows also leave a traceless path, so he decided there was no contradiction there. *Maybe I'm missing the point. I know the sky is used as a metaphor for the mind, so this is probably just supposed to be about what happens in the mind.* He imagined things like hatred and attachment moving through his mind like birds through the sky. *Could they simply disappear on their own power, leaving a traceless path? Then what's the deal about not getting absorbed in experience? Is experience traceless too?*

He put the book down on his dresser, left his room, and walked down the hallway and the flight of stairs, debating whether or not experience leaves a trace. And if it leaves a trace, then where would it be found? *Maybe experience is like an empty bowl of time until it's filled with things like feelings and actions—oh, yeah—and ripening karma too. No. Wait. It can't just be an empty bowl of time, otherwise everyone would be having the same experience in the same moments of time. And if experience exists in time, then we wouldn't be able to recall certain experiences so vividly at another time. So, experience must be something that happens in the mind.*

How Patience Works

Troy then thought more about attachment and hatred, two of the Three Poisons. *Maybe they don't leave a trace by themselves, but if you don't know better, both physical actions and actions of thought and speech will come from them. Then that strengthens the mind's habits of hatred and attachment, and it creates more negative karma. Then those habits will show up as a result of karmic imprints like the stains on the teacup Abe talked about, and then, in that same way, they just keep showing up time after time. So the only trace must be the karmic imprints on that most subtle mind Mrs. Sternau described.*

As if his brain couldn't handle moving while thinking so hard at the same time, he stopped midway down the stairs when something more came to mind. *So the advice to not be absorbed in experience must be because you'll be drawn into believing an experience is more concrete than it really is. If you don't get that it's actually empty of anything except ripening karma, then you might do something stupid like become violent if you're angry or want something so badly that you lie or steal in order to get it. And then those actions set up the karma for your next scene.* He continued on down the stairs and out the front door, mulling these things over in his mind.

He was startled out of his thoughts when a car horn blasted long and loud while he was opening the door to his truck. He turned to see Maureen's car fish-tailing as it sped into the driveway. It was dark enough that Troy couldn't see Maureen's face clearly, but he was fairly certain it wasn't going to be pretty. It was hard to tell what happened first, the engine turning off as the car slammed into park or the door opening with Maureen springing out like an angry bull loose from its gate.

"I hate you!" she screamed. "You low-life thief, I hate your goddamn guts!" She shoved the car door closed with so much force it might as well have been made of solid cast iron, and she marched toward him armed with fury. "This is my house and my garden, and those were my goddamn flowers that you stole, you goddamn bastard." Her face was red, and Troy could see every line and crease clearly as it was now within a foot of his own just before her arm reached back to slap him. It was the sound he heard first—it sounded like a whip—and then the sting he felt burning on his cheek before she turned and ran toward the house.

The slap dulled his sense of sound, and Troy stood in the dim light with the muted chirping of crickets, bringing his hand to hold the area on his face she had hit.

"I'm sorry." He spoke loudly enough to be sure she could hear him. *Karma ripening,* he reminded himself, thinking of the empty bowl of experience. He thought of the many fights he'd been in but mostly the one when he hit the other guy's face so hard he thought he'd killed him. The image of seeing him lying unconscious flashed its nightmare in his mind. *Let the anger fly on its own power, leaving no trace. This experience is empty until I add something to it. I'm so done with all of this. If I let this karma ripen without creating more of the same, I'm actually changing the cycle. If Abe and Professor Sternau could do it, so can I. It's in dependence on Maureen that I will find peace. I know what to do.*

"I'm really sorry, Maureen," he said before she got inside. "I thought it was okay. My mistake." *Not my mistake with the flowers, but so many mistakes in the past.* He felt blood trickling down his neck. Her nails must have scratched his face. He looked on the seat of his truck for paper or a cloth he could use to blot the blood and found a napkin. It wasn't a lot of blood, but he checked in the side mirror of his truck just to see. There was a mark on his face and a scratch by his ear. He wasn't fazed. He had been hurt worse than this before.

When he looked up again, Maureen was standing in the driveway, hands on her hips. "You thought it was okay?" She hurled her pocketbook toward him, but instead it swung around and spilled its entire contents by her feet. Infuriated even more, she picked up a tube of lipstick and threw it at him, but her aim was far from perfect. "How the hell can you ever think it's okay to take something without asking?"

"You're right," he said. "I'm really, really sorry, Maureen."

"All the women from my garden club are coming for a luncheon tomorrow, and now my garden looks like shit." She gathered everything that had spilled back into her purse and stomped furiously into the house.

Impressing the women in her garden club was one of Maureen's obsessions. Troy wished he had Professor Sternau's gardening skills so he could easily fix whatever disaster the missing roses and daisies had left behind. Since it was clear whatever he said made things worse, there was nothing more for him to say.

He called Maggie to let her know something had come up with Maureen. He apologized for being late and told her he was on his way. When she pressed him to tell her what happened, he said he'd tell her once he

How Patience Works

got there. His next phone call was to Theo. He needed to have the following day off, and he asked if someone else could take his breakfast and lunch shifts. Troy had never missed work, and Theo could tell by the tone in Troy's voice that he wouldn't be asking if it weren't important. He liked Troy and wanted to help him out. He said he was confident someone would take the shift and not to worry about it.

~

If I become angry with the wielder,
Although I am actually harmed by the stick,
Then since the perpetrator, too, is secondary, being in
turn incited by hatred,
I should be angry with the hatred instead.

Previously, I must have caused similar harm
To other sentient beings.
Therefore, it is right for this harm to be returned
To me, who caused injury to others.
VI. 41, 42

Troy set his alarm for five o'clock and wasn't even tempted to hit the snooze button when it went off the next morning. His plan was to be out the door before anyone else was out of bed. Feeling the tightness in his calves from running, he limped quietly into the bathroom to splash water on his face. From his unmade bed, he took a blanket and folded it into a cushion to help support his back while he meditated. Once seated, he settled into his posture and then tried to settle his mind. It was hard to not be drawn into revisiting the conversation he'd had with Maggie. She was outraged by what Maureen had done. She said Maureen had crossed the line from verbal and emotional abuse into physical abuse, and that none of it should ever be tolerated. She didn't understand Troy's passivity in the face of abuse or why he didn't just tell his father what had happened so he could straighten Maureen out. Of course Troy would have defended and protected himself if necessary. He didn't feel his safety was at risk, but rather that the things he was striving to correct in his own life were. If he told his father what happened, then he would only create another conflict and another reason for Maureen to experience anger.

He was observing the circumstances in his life the way an archaeologist might examine objects discovered on a dig to explain the mysteries of the past. He remembered Mrs. Sternau saying that it takes awhile for our outer world to catch up with our inner world, and so it wasn't surprising to experience negative results from his past actions. He tried to tell Maggie, but his words inadequately conveyed just how strongly he felt there was a direct connection between his own violence and the slap he received from Maureen. Even more difficult to explain was the compassion he felt for Maureen. Maggie could only see that he had been hurt and that Maureen was abusive. Troy wished Maggie could understand that Maureen's self-centered worldview was one that held her separate and apart from the happiness she wanted most. There wasn't a house big enough, or enough jewelry, or husband, or any number of friends who could fill the hole her loneliness and fear had dug. He told Maggie that there is no enemy except for ignorance. Therefore, Maureen wasn't his enemy, nor was he hers.

He relaxed his shoulders and let them drop with neither shoulder higher than the other. By raising the top of his head toward the ceiling, he drew his spine straight, not leaning backward or forward; something he had a tendency to do if he wasn't paying attention. He kept his arms relaxed and rested the back of his right hand within the palm of his left, thumbs touching lightly together and just in front of his lower abdomen.

He then lowered his eyes so that his gaze was at the floor just about two feet in front of him. He focused his mind on his breath and began counting each round of breath's inhalation through its exhalation. The goal was to reach ten cycles of breath without his mind wandering. He seldom made it past five or six, and there were days when even reaching three was impossible. Each time his focus wandered, he began counting again from one. His strong motivation this morning was to make sure all his actions during the day would stem from a compassionate, clear, and steady mind.

Gradually his breathing became quieter and slower, and his mind became less agitated. When imaginary conversations between Maureen and himself or with his dad began their inner chatter, he pictured the traceless flight of birds and let them wing lightly through his mind without landing to roost. Soon his body, mind, and breath felt in perfect unison, gently moving only with the soft rhythm of each breath. The sensation reminded him of the peace he felt floating in the ocean, the water holding him weightless beneath his back, while the sun poured its warm light into each pore of his body. Stabilizing his mind this way through his breathing, he then concentrated on a point of light he visualized in front of himself level with his forehead.

Other people might choose to imagine a saint, someone they admire deeply, a great prophet, or Buddha, or Christ, but Troy was more comfortable with a point of light that he designed in his mind to represent great compassion, ultimate truth, and love.

He recalled the discussion he and Grace had when she told him that as long as there are people and other beings that are suffering there can be no real peace. Grace said that when you really understand this, your reflexive response to seeing someone in pain is to offer compassion. She used an analogy that made a lot of sense to Troy when she explained that if you have a pain in your foot, then your hand immediately reaches to hold it or massage it to relieve its discomfort. The hand never thinks, "oh—forget about that foot—it's not my problem..." Grace said that when we truly comprehend just how interconnected all beings are, our response to others' pain is similar to that of the hand toward the foot.

Grace wasn't only referring to physical pain. She was talking about the pain that comes from ignorance. Ignorance is like pollution dumped into a river, carrying toxins and destruction downstream. The pollution of ignorance in the mind shows up in the toxicity of anger, greed, jealousy, conceit, fear, and anxiety, just to name a few of the many forms ignorance can take. They in turn trigger destructive actions with more negative results.

We all share the experience of ripening karma, and we have a choice as to whether we will respond in ways to either stop the cycle of pain and suffering or perpetuate it. Grace said that when our understanding of interdependence becomes as obvious and clear to us as our understanding of the laws of gravity, then peace is possible. By knowing the laws of gravity, we rush to catch a child before he or she falls, and by knowing the truth of our interdependence, our impulse to offer compassion to someone suffering from any form of ignorance will be equally reflexive. Sometimes we need to be reminded to offer compassion to ourselves as well.

Grace explained that with practice, it is possible for this understanding to develop into something called enlightenment-mind or bodhicitta. It is a very powerful state of mind that has a transformative power to convert disharmony into peace, and it carries the intention to seek enlightenment for the benefit of all sentient beings.

It was a preliminary understanding of interdependence and compassion that supported Troy's mind for quite some time as he held his focus on the point of light, his breathing calm and steady. As he breathed softly and freely, he imagined he breathed for everyone whose breathing was compromised by illness and that his breathing might ease theirs. Sitting in the quiet comfort of his room, he imagined those who have no home, or live in very rough conditions, to meet the causes and conditions for comfortable and safe shelter. He thought of those living in areas where food and water are scarce, and he imagined serving them plates of delicious food and pitchers filled with clean water. He thought about all who live in violence and imagined their world at peace. Before he left his meditation, he dedicated the positive value of his practice to benefit all sentient beings and to support his determination to keep his mind focused on love and compassion.

Troy walked quietly down the stairs and out the back door to assess the damage where he had cut the flowers in the garden. He tried to imagine how the garden might look if seen through Maureen's view of perfection. Even in the early light, he could see that the flowers he cut, especially the roses, left a chunk of space where color was missing. He needed to find something to fill that space.

Maggie would know an effective way to help camouflage the missing color. She knew all about things like directing the eyes' focus through use of color. But it was too early to call, and, besides, Maggie was so angry with Maureen, she had no tolerance for her or for her concerns about impressing the ladies from the garden club. Troy had another idea. His friend Kyle worked for a landscaper. Kyle would know what to do.

Thus since sentient beings have a share
In giving rise to the supreme Buddha-qualities,
Surely it is correct to venerate them
As they are similar in merely this respect?

Furthermore, what way is there to repay (the Buddhas)
Who grant immeasurable benefit
And who befriend the world without pretension,
Other than by pleasing sentient beings?
VI. 118, 119

Troy checked the time. It was nearly six o'clock. Landscapers always start their work early. He was sure

Kyle would be up soon if not already. Troy got into his truck and drove away from the house before calling Kyle. The call went right to voice mail. "Damn," he said, hanging up without leaving a message. Not sure where to go first, he followed the roads that led into town. He pulled into the drive-thru line for coffee at the corner bagel and donut shop. With his plan still forming, it seemed as good a destination as any. He sat in line, waiting his turn to place an order, when his phone rang.

"Thank God," Troy said when he saw Kyle's name show up. "Dude, I need your help." He didn't tell him all the details, but just enough about the situation so Kyle would get an idea what was needed. Admittedly, there was an absurdity to the story as he heard himself tell it. He listened to some of Kyle's more sarcastic suggestions before Kyle finally got around to telling him to meet him at the wholesale nursery.

"It's where all the landscapers buy their plants," Kyle said. "I can get you a good deal on a nice climbing rose or something like that. I was just there yesterday. They've got 'em in a lot of different colors. I'll meet you there in an hour."

"An hour?" Troy asked. "What am I gonna do for an hour? I can't go back to the house yet."

"I don't know," Kyle said. "Just drive around and enjoy your coffee and the sunrise or something."

So he drove the road that led to the woods and took the turn down Mrs. Sternau's road. He had worried about her after he and Maggie left, and he hoped a nap truly was all she had needed. He drove slowly past the houses—some still with porch lights lit and their blinds drawn. Others showed signs of morning activity. He saw a man, already dressed for work, open his door to take the newspaper from his walkway. Troy drove a little further. Sipping his coffee, it splashed from the lid when his tires rolled bumpily over a pothole. As he approached Mrs. Sternau's house, he remembered her saying she's up with the birds each morning, so he was relieved to see her front door open and the kitchen light on.

He found her number stored in his phone and called. The phone rang four times before she answered. "Hello?"

What if it's too early to call? "Good morning, Mrs. Sternau. It's Troy. I'm sorry to be calling so early."

"Ah yes, good morning. Is it early?" she asked. "I've been up for quite some time and have already begun my puzzle."

"I'm in the neighborhood and wanted to know if it's okay to stop by to take another look at your porch door," he said. *No shit, Sherlock. You're not in the neighborhood; you're practically in her driveway already.* "But I don't want to interrupt you if this isn't a good time."

"Oh, the crossword puzzle isn't going anywhere, and there's nothing to interrupt," she reassured him. "Please come on over. I'll be happy to see you."

Troy waited a few minutes before driving on so it wouldn't be obvious that he was already so close. Mrs. Sternau was standing at the door waiting for him when he walked up the path to her house. "Good morning, dear," she said. "What a pleasant surprise to hear from you this morning. Come in, please. Would you like some coffee?"

"Um, sure. Thank you," Troy said.

In the kitchen, she took a cup and saucer from the cupboard and poured steaming coffee from the percolator that reflected rays of sun like cartooned starlight. He carried the coffee into the room where he and Maggie had left her the day before and sat in the armchair by the window. In the morning brightness that filled the room, the mark on his face from Maureen's slap was visible.

"My heavens, what is that on your face?" Mrs. Sternau asked.

It was hard to know where to begin. So rather than start at the beginning Troy started at the end, including Maggie's reaction, and worked his way back.

Mrs. Sternau listened quietly while Troy spoke. Once he finished, she told him that not only was he proving to be an excellent student, but someone with exceptional courage. She studied her husband's photograph on the table next to Troy. "Courage like yours is a result of a strong conviction that does not doubt the way karma works or the wisdom of true compassion. Maggie's concerns about tolerating abuse are perfectly understandable, and unless you are some kind of enlightened being in disguise, it is not recommended to permit someone to cause you harm. That being said, with a great deal of practice and wisdom, one can eventually learn to stop a harmful action with no thought of anger arising. This is ideal, and while of course it's not easy to do, with the practice of mindfulness it can be done. Parents can be good examples of something like this when their child is about to do something dangerous like run into a busy road. They might use what appears to be a rough intervention in order to protect the child. But it is not done with anger. It is only love for their child that fills their mind."

Mrs. Sternau interrupted herself. "Oh gracious, you need to meet your friend soon. There is always so much to talk about; you mustn't let me get carried away just now. The porch door can wait. You need to be on your way shortly, and I have something in mind that would go perfectly with the plant you will buy for your stepmother. If you begin digging and planting in your stepmother's garden, she will become even angrier. What you must do is buy a plant that can stay in its container and then, after her luncheon, she can choose to have it planted wherever she likes."

Mrs. Sternau stood from the sofa. "Follow me, darling. I have a fabulous idea." Without waiting for Troy to settle his coffee cup in its saucer, she took her cane with such purpose she might have used it to part the sea. Out the porch door and down the steps, Troy walked with Mrs. Sternau to the lattice door that opened to a low space beneath the porch. "This is where Albert kept his gardening tools and pots for planting." She used her cane to point as she said, "There, in the far corner, dear, can you make your way over to that collection of pots?"

Inside, it was a dirt floor, and all the tools and whatnot were coated with layers of dust. The ceiling was too low for Troy to stand, so he bent and strained to see what was piled in the corner. "There're lots of pots back here, Mrs. Sternau. Anything in particular you want me to look for?"

"Yes. I'm hoping you can find a porcelain pot Albert used on our patio for summer decorating. He stored it here through the winter, after the plants died in the fall, until the spring. It was a gift from the Lanimakers, and I simply never got around to taking it out again after he died."

"Is this it?" Troy asked. He picked up a heavy container and held it out for Mrs. Sternau to see.

"Oh, marvelous! Yes, it is," she said. "Can you please bring it out?"

"Okay." Troy rolled it along the edge of its base to the door and then onto the path where Mrs. Sternau stood. He didn't know much about antiques, but thought it looked like some of the pieces Abe kept in his apartment, and even some of the nicer pieces in his shop. The colors were dulled beneath layers of dust and dirt, but it could clean up nicely.

"The Lanimakers brought this from China, and I've plumb forgotten all about it until it suddenly popped in my mind while we were upstairs talking. Its size is deep enough that you should be able to buy a fairly tall rose plant and slip it, planter and all, inside."

"This looks like it might be a valuable antique. Are you sure you want me to take it? Maureen will think I'm giving it to her."

"Well, you are giving it to her. For heaven's sake, I have no use for it. It's been cooped up in this crawl space for over twenty years. It's high time it had an ornamental place of beauty in someone's garden." She straightened a pin that was coming loose from her hair and secured the twist she hadn't yet arranged for the day. "Now, let's get it scrubbed and beautiful before you leave." Again, she used her cane to direct Troy—this time toward the outdoor faucet. "Now, take it over there, and then I want you to run inside to my laundry room where you will find a scrub brush and some detergent." She told him where the laundry room was and asked him to also bring two old towels she kept on a shelf for cleaning. "Don't walk at my pace, dearie, or it will take all day. You go ahead and move quickly."

Troy carried the pot over to the faucet and lowered it carefully to the ground. Cobwebs, dried leaves, and dead insects had accumulated in its bottom, but in the light he could see that, once cleaned, it would be a piece Maureen might be proud to own. He jogged up the steps to the porch and into the house. Down the hallway, next to the garage, he found the laundry room, the jug of detergent, a scrub brush, and the towels, all just as she described. On his way back through the porch he found a light chair to carry along so Mrs. Sternau could sit.

Mrs. Sternau sat a distance from the spray of the hose, and watched as Troy scrubbed the dirt and stains from the pot. She had suggested they share this activity together by using it as a mindfulness meditation. "Darling, we can train ourselves to bring mindfulness to everything we do. Things like how we listen to others, how we speak, and how we engage in the moment by moments throughout our day. As you wash the vase, let's imagine the water and detergent to be love and compassion purifying all negativities of anger and hatred that have left stains in our minds, your step-mother's mind, and the minds of all sentient beings."

Troy found that the dirt washed away easily, but he took his time giving careful attention to all the curves and surfaces. He imagined his mind and heart being polished clean and Maureen's sparkling like the diamond she wore in her ring. He didn't know how it was possible to picture all other sentient beings, so when an image of light blanketing the planet came to mind, he went with that. As he toweled the vase dry, he noticed the deeper detail of the green vines, a pair of butterflies, and flush rose blossoms that gently patterned their way around its shape. And when he sensed that Mrs. Sternau had finished her own meditation, he asked her what color roses she thought he should buy.

"You know, my eyesight isn't as good as it once was," she said. "And I'm sure there are subtle shades of colors in the vase that you can see better than I." The heat of the day drew steamy wisps from puddles dissolving into the gravel path, and the air smelled earth sweet. "Ruth always said that if colors are found together in nature, then you can trust they complement each other nicely in other settings. I suggest you simply look at what's available, and you'll recognize the loveliest when you see it."

Once everything was put away and the pot loaded safely in the truck, Mrs. Sternau wished Troy success and watched as he backed from her driveway. Just before Troy turned out of view he stopped to wave. Through the shade of the screen, for a brief second, she looked very young.

There is nothing whatsoever
That is not made easier through acquaintance.
So through becoming acquainted with small harms,
I should learn to patiently accept greater harms.

Who has not seen this to be so, with trifling sufferings
Such as the bites of snakes and insects,
Feelings of hunger and thirst,
And with such minor things as rashes?

I should not be impatient
With heat and cold, wind and rain,
Sickness, bondage and beatings;
For if I am, the harm they cause me will increase.
VI. 14, 15, 16

The morning activity at the nursery was unfamiliar to Troy, but he thought if he had more time he would have enjoyed staying there. The air smelled good, and the sounds were busy but purposeful. Motorized sprinklers clicked and dragged, rotating to spray long beams of water. Tailgates creaked and slammed after trees with roots balled in burlap were loaded into pickup beds.

Men were speaking Spanish amid lots of laughter, but Troy didn't understand anything they were saying. There were rows and rows of trees and shrubs, and everyone seemed to know his way around, but Troy didn't see anyone who looked in charge of helping.

Troy checked his phone for messages and then for the time. It was getting late, and Maureen was probably getting ready to take Natalie to school. After so many snow days, the school year was extended and still in session for Natalie. Troy had hoped to have everything in place and to be gone from the house before Maureen got back, but it looked like that might not happen. He tried calling Kyle. Again, there was no answer. There was no time to waste, so he walked along the rows, scanning them for signs of flowering plants.

Then his phone rang. It was Kyle. "Troy. Dude, where are you? I just pulled in next to your truck."

"Stay there. I'll come meet you," Troy said, jogging with sore legs toward where he had parked. "Thank God you're here. I need your help big time."

Kyle was leaning against the front of Troy's truck when he got there. Troy opened the door. "Take a look at this," he showed Kyle the pot. "We've gotta find something that will fit in it and look really good, okay?"

"You want a rose, right?" Kyle asked.

"Yeah," Troy said. "It's gotta be roses. And it's gotta be fast."

"You got it. Come with me," Kyle said.

Kyle cut across the lot, past the shed that was the office and place to pay for purchases. They walked past a collection of lawn decorations, birdbaths, and ceramic angels and gnomes. He noticed the smell of roses before he saw them. He never knew there were so many colors and breeds, but he knew he didn't have time for a complicated decision. The roses he had cut were red so he decided to stay with red.

"Okay, red it is." Kyle led him to the next row. "Take your pick."

Troy found a plant that was nicely formed; the flowers were red but slightly smaller than those he had cut. It was in a black plastic container that would easily fit in the pot Mrs. Sternau had given him. "This is it," he said. "I'll take this one."

The man behind the counter knew Kyle, who introduced him to Troy. Kyle and the man talked casually about some new products that work well and some that don't or aren't worth the money. Every moment of conversation, exchanging money, waiting for the cash register to open, for the paper to feed and the receipt to print, stretched into an agonizing eternity as Troy felt the race against time. Finally, the sale was complete.

"Kyle, thank you. I'll let you know how it goes, but I've gotta run," Troy said as he carried the rose toward the door. "Nice meeting you," he said to the man behind the register.

"Later, dude," Kyle said.

Just to check the fit, he put the rose plant inside the pot the way Mrs. Sternau said it should go. "Perfect," he whispered with relief. With that in place he climbed into the truck. As he slammed the door shut, he noticed his mind racing everywhere but to where he was and to what he was actually doing. Before he turned the key in the ignition, he reminded himself to use his breath to pull his mind back into a more calm, present, and focused state. Otherwise, nothing he was going to do would go nearly as well. After all he had learned first hand, he knew this for a fact. Grace said that since it's always with us, the breath is the perfect object in meditation to bring one's attention to, and the more you practice, the more readily you can work with it. He closed his eyes, took his hand off the key, and as his breathing slowed, so did the racing of his thoughts. It was becoming more evident just how closely linked his mind was to his breathing and to all other symptoms of stress. His practice was paying off, and it didn't take long for him to bring his mind back to the focus he'd set his intention to earlier that morning. Holding love, wisdom, and compassion in the center of his mind like the hub of a wheel touching the earth with each turn of its spokes, he made his way across town and back to his house.

There is no doubt that those with
the nature of compassion
Regard all these beings (the same) as themselves.
Furthermore, those who see (this Buddha nature)
as the nature
of sentient beings also see the Buddhas themselves;
Why then do I not respect (sentient beings)?

(Pleasing living beings) delights the Tathagatas[5]
And perfectly accomplishes my own purpose as well.
In addition, it dispels the pain and misery of the
universe,
Therefore I should always practice it.
VI. 126, 127

---

5   One who has attained enlightenment.

Troy's father had already left for work, and Maureen hadn't yet returned from taking Natalie to school. Troy hoped she might stop at the grocery store or do other errands, buying him extra time to get things in place and to be on his way before she got home. He took the plant in its new pot from the truck and carried it to the back of the house, around the deck, and to the spot in the garden that was to be its new home. Or at least its new home for the day. He placed the pot on the lawn while he evaluated the contour of the flowerbed and how it would best be positioned. He looked more carefully at the design on the pot to see if any portion was more appealing than another. Turning it so the butterflies appeared to be flying in from the left, he nudged the pot onto the soil by the gardens' edge. He slid the plastic planter around until the fullest portion of the plant with the most blooms was facing outward. He took a few steps back to look first from the left, and then from the right. Looking over the entire garden, Troy noticed that it didn't have the flowing lines and quaint charm of Mrs. Sternau's garden, but it was in some way more geometric and symmetrical with a more contemporary garden-catalog feel. The rose plant in the antique pot added an interesting juxtaposition of design that Troy thought was both tasteful and striking. And the smaller roses in the pot set in front of the larger ones behind it added a nice texture.

He was about to leave when he remembered the day Abe talked about the importance of dedication before they gave Rich the money they found. He told Troy to consider their generosity was an act that could purify his negative karma—like cleanser for the tea stains in the cup—and also an offering to benefit others. He said to cultivate his most heartfelt wish for every single being throughout the entire universe to be free from suffering and its causes and to have happiness and its causes. Troy wanted to do something similar before he left the flowers and the pot for Maureen.

He tried to remember the prayers the minister used to say when he was a kid and his parents took him to church. There was a time during the church service when baskets would be passed around through the congregation. People would drop money into the baskets, and then the baskets would be carried, full of money, to the front of the church. The organist always seemed to know when they were getting ready to bring the money forward and would begin playing big, dramatic chords. Troy used to wish he could sit where the organist sat and watch how he played while working all the pedals and knobs at the same time. If he hadn't been so intrigued by the organist and all the activity of the people carrying the baskets all so perfectly timed, he might have been able to remember the prayerful words the minister said when he offered the collection.

Rough as it might have been, Troy came up with his own form of prayer and dedication that came authentically from his heart. But it was an awkward start. *Um, I offer this plant and beautiful pot from Mrs. Sternau for Maureen's happiness and, uhhhm, so she can be free from the awful agony that holds her in such a state of fear and hostility. Uuuhh, let's see, what else? I also dedicate this offering so I can be free from the ignorance that is the cause of all suffering. And with a strong wish for all beings throughout the entire universe to be at peace, to be free from all suffering and all causes of suffering and to have only happiness and causes of happiness. May I be a source of wisdom and compassion for all others and never cause harm to anyone ever again. Really. Please. Never again. Um… and, uhh… how does that thing go with the bees? So much depends on the bees…. Like Professor Sternau said, it's on their wings we'll spread the pollen of love and compassion or else of anger and hatred. Wow, it really is like a garden, isn't it? If I can be free of all seeds of anger,*

*then I will never grow or germinate pain and suffering
for myself or anyone else again. That's why Maureen
is such a precious gem—because I absolutely feel no
anger whatsoever. Oh my God, I can't believe this. I
really don't feel any anger at all. How lucky am I? It's
like I really, really love her. Wow—it's kinda weird, but
I do.* The awareness that he felt no anger was pivotal.
He felt an immediate and powerful sense of gratitude
and a stinging in his eyes as tears began to swell until he
heard the sound of Maureen's car door closing.

*I'm not running away. But I'm not gonna track her
down either—she doesn't want to see me.* He picked
up a twig that had fallen onto the lawn and then bent
to adjust the pot, wriggling it a little more evenly into
the soil. When he stood, Maureen was standing on
the lawn. She stopped walking just a few feet from
him. Eyes meeting, neither one said a word. Maureen
looked at the pot and then the new plant. She noticed
its flowers filling the space left by the others Troy had
cut. Her eyes traced the leaves back down to the pot
and settled there, taking in the uniqueness of its design.
She looked at Troy and winced at the mark on his face
and the scab near his ear. Troy thought he heard her
breath tighten like a short gasp before she walked over
to the pot and crouched to see it more closely. With

one hand touching the porcelain, following the green of the vines with fingers spread open tentatively, the other hand gently lowering her purse off her shoulder to the ground. She stood, keeping her back to Troy.

"You've done it again," she said.

Troy waited to hear what he had done this time. Her voice was tense but low.

"I don't get it. How do you do this? *Why* do you do this? You stand there wearing my wretchedness like a goddamn mirror on your face for me to see, and then you bring this—this—this beautiful planter and rose plant as if it were you who had done something wrong." She still wouldn't turn to look at him. "Your dad told me that it was him. That he was the one who told you to cut the flowers." She was quiet.

"They're beautiful, Troy. The flowers are beautiful, and this pot is fabulous—it looks like an antique, and it's gorgeous." Troy heard the bees in the clover and watched them while she spoke. "I can't look at you, Troy, because I'll cry, and I can't cry because once I start I might not stop, and I've got company coming, and if they see me crying then they'll want to know why, and I can't tell anyone why because I don't know what's the matter with me, and… I just need help." She gulped three fast breaths. "I need help, Troy." She turned to face Troy, with tears filling her eyes so they looked like scared fish eyes in water. She reached her arms and threw them and all her sorrow around him. "I need your help, Troy," she said almost in a whisper.

"No more than I need yours," Troy answered.

My Darling Albert,

There is so much to delight in this morning I can barely contain myself, but why ever would I want to? There is unsurpassed beauty in the garden as it pulses with its gentle power and is absolutely radiant in its peace. Our young man has taken the pot where it is being put to its intended use. We knew the time would come darling. Yes, we knew the time would come. And so it has, and so it is.

Loving you always,
Esther

How Patience Works

Hence everything is governed by other factors
(which in turn) are governed by (others),
And in this way nothing governs itself.
Having understood this, I should not become angry
With phenomena, which are like apparitions.

(If everything is unreal, like an apparition,) then who
is there to restrain what (anger)?
Surely (in this case) restraint would be inappropriate—
It would not be inappropriate, because
(conventionally) I must maintain
That in dependence upon restraining (anger), the
stream of suffering is severed.

So when one sees an enemy or even a friend
Committing an improper action,
By thinking that such things arise from conditions
I shall remain in a happy frame of mind.

If things were brought into being by choice,
Then since no one wishes to suffer,
Suffering would not occur
To any embodied creature.
VI. 31,32, 33, 34

Acknowledgments

It is impossible for me to even imagine writing this book without the teachings I have had the good fortune and honor to receive from the monks at Do Ngak Kunphen Ling in Redding, Connecticut. I wish to thank Gyumed Khensur Lobsang Jampa, Geshe Lobsang Dhargey, Geshe Tashi, Jampa Gyeltsen, Thupten Phuntsok, Gelek Lodo, Datemba Sherpa, and Lobsang Sherab for their kindness, patience, and generosity in sharing the dharma teachings and practice, and for demonstrating the way of the Bodhisattva.

An especially heartfelt thank you to Jeff Fookson for allowing me to borrow from his own family's experience to set the stage for Professor and Mrs. Sternau in *How Patience Works*. Nearly twenty years ago, Jeff told me his father had been accused of being a communist sympathizer by Joseph McCarthy's committee during what is now known as the McCarthy era. His father had written a letter of recommendation for a friend who was later revealed to be on McCarthy's list of suspected communists. Through this association, accusations were made, and Jeff's father was forced to leave his job. I never forgot the story, and I never forgot the painful and lasting imprint it left on Jeff and his entire family.

My continued appreciation and gratitude to John Cerullo and Clare Cerullo at Karuna Publications. John holds the guiding vision to demonstrate the relevance of Master Shantideva's teachings in contemporary life throughout The How Life Works series. His unwavering confidence encourages me to write, persevering through the moments when my own ability to comprehend a topic feels out of reach. As an editor, Clare fine-tunes the text with grace and sensitivity that is rooted in her own study of the subject matter. As an artist, she designs a book that has both an aesthetic and tactile quality of something sacred.

And last but certainly not least, my deepest thanks to my sons Geoffrey and Daniel, the loving inspiration that pours through everything I do.